KNOCKING ABOUT

Gus Pierce

ETT IMPRINT

Exile Bay

First published by ETT Imprint, Exile Bay 2021

First published by Yale University as by Augustus Baker Peirce, 1924
Facsimile edition by Shoestring Press, 1984
First electronic edition ETT Imprint 2021

Compiled by Tom Thompson

ETT IMPRINT
PO Box R1906
Royal Exchange NSW 1225
Australia

ISBN 978-1-922473-58-5 (paper)
ISBN 978-1-922473-59-2 (ebook)

Design by Hanna Gotlieb
Cover by Tom Thompson

Photographs of Bathurst and Hill End all by Beaufoy Merlin.
Cover: Gus Pierce's troupe outside the Theatre Royal, Hill End 1872

The publisher is grateful for the help of Heather Rendle at the Echuca
Historical Society, Gordon Dowell and Lorraine Purcell for their help in
the gathering of details on the author's life

CONTENTS

Captain Gus Pierce, as photographed by Beaufoy Merlin at Hill End in 1872.

INTRODUCTION

Augustus Baker Peirce arrived in Australia the "traditional" way – swimming ashore in Port Philip Bay after deserting the US Naval ship, the *Oriental* in 1860. As keen as other American dreamers like Freeman Cobb of Cobb & Co; let loose in the new country, he threw himself at any occupation before finding a livelihood as a photographer, artist and theatrical entrepreneur.

For over thirty years Peirce embarked on showing Australians their new land, whether it be by his remarkable survey of the Murray River for the steamer trade , or taking them through vast painted panoramas showing the gold diggings, Aboriginals, and the stark beauty and remarkable features of South Australia, Victoria and New South Wales. His vision was bold and his manner of sweet talking was reminiscent of writer Mark Twain, whose greatest dream was to captain a paddle-steamer.

From the outset, Peirce realised his surname was being read as "Pierce", and he began signing his work and acting as "Gus B. Pierce". His marriage and two sons were also called Pierce. So for the purposes of this book, he will be "Pierce" throughout.

Pierce used his American connections to get work with Benjamin Batchelder, originally Batchelder and O'Neill of Salem, Massachusetts – and worked in Bendigo for them, being instructed in scene painting there by John Fry of the Lyceum Theatre. He began a pantomime group known as 'Gus B. Pierce, the great American Delineator and Serio-Comic Lecturer' which was not sucesssful; Gus was simply way ahead of his time.

He was fascinated with Australian fauna, and caught snakes with Joe Shires, of Snake-bite Cure fame. He was absorbed with studying Aboriginals, and while his photographs are lost, there are examples of his drawings within this book.

When Yale University first published *Knocking About* in 1924, many local readers were confused by his constant name-changing, and the miss-spelling of people he had met, like members of the "Kelley" Gang. For the purposes of this book we have corrected these, along with his mistaken dates for his marriage, wife's death and departure; providing a timeline to help the reader battle with the constant movement of Pierce "on the road" in Australia.

For many, Pierce lived several lives – captaining several grand steamers on the Murray River; presenting his hand-painted panoramas in three States; his theatre presentations and stand-up comedy act of being an American in the new Australian "woods"; and his later sedate life as a painter of horses and Melbourne scenes.

In 1863 Gus Pierce surveyed the Murray from Albury to Goolwa - a 1750 mile journey, with an Aboriginal tracker and a Dancing Master named Everest, who job was to dance a Welcome to Country on each side of the river as they surveyed through Aboriginal tribal lands. He later became Captain on several steamboats, from 1864 to 1876, including *Lady Daly, Corowa, Jane Eliza, Victoria* and *Riverina*.

By 1869 he was creating immense panoramas on rollers, several over 200 feet long, perhaps emulating his Murray survey chart. As the newspapers said of this first panorama: 'A peep of a remarkable portion of the Lower Murray and a view of a tributary of the same stream are interesting and in both the water and foliage of the trees and bushes are capitally painted.'

Gus Pierce toured Victoria and New South Wales with his panorama during 1870-71, while painting murals for hotels. He created a travelling show of murals with musical accompaniment to

Wagga Wagga, playing Gulgong in 1871. The review in the *Gulgong Guardian* (July 15) said: "Captain Pierce's Panorama. This amusing and instructive entertainment opened at Cogdon's Assembly Rooms on Thursday last, before a tolerably filled house. The panorama comprises views of places historical and geographical interest, in various parts of the globe, and each picture has been painted with considerable artistic taste. The Port Philip Heads is a very striking view, and the lights in the lighthouse and on board ship, and the glittering of the moonlight on the water, gives to the picture a life-like reality... The singing of Mr. Wood, and the excellent comic singing of Captain Gus Pierce, also brought down the house. Captain Pierce's lecture is one of the cleverest, in its way, that we have listened to for many a day, and the laughter it drew from the audience was frequent and hearty. The Captain is an eloquent "talkist," his wit being of the American school, and we advise all who suffer from lowness of spirits to go and hear him. The panorama will stay here for some few nights longer, and we can promise those who visit it a pleasant evening's enjoyment."

In 1872 he first showed lantern slides and his paintings & theatricals at Hill End in a huge tent in the main street of Hill End - The Theatre Royal with a Canadian actor William B Gill, and put on a Varieties show called *Jumpers of Hill End*. With the discovery of Holtermann's great nugget of gold in October, Pierce was commissioned by Bernard Holtermann to create a new 200 foot panorama *A Mirror of Life*, and offered him a studio at this Star of Hope mine. Thus Pierce is the first artist at Hill End, preceding Donald Friend and Russell Drysdale by 70 years.

Holtermann had already commissioned the photographers Beaufoy Merlin and Charles Bayliss to photograph Gulgong, Home Rule, and Hill End, and this remarkable record we can now see features several images of Pierce and Gill, noted on the cover and within this book. We can also see that Pierce's son Augustus, is with him in Hill End, and that this was a relatively stable period for "The Great American Delineator".

Pierce already had his fans, as noted in the *Riverina Herald* (7 December 1872) *Hill End Times and Tambaroora Advocate*):

By the following paragraph from (Hill End), we learn that a gentleman well known in Adelaide, and still more so on the Murray, has transferred his talents and varied accomplishments to the most flourishing of the New South Wales gold-fields: – "We must congratulate Gus Pierce upon the admirable manner in which with his facile brush and inventive powers he has conferred beauty on the wall of Dodd's Hotel, Clarke Street. He has portioned off the walls of the bar, parlors, &c, into panels, upon which he has depicted with great skill a variety of beautiful objects. Over the door leading from the bar into the passage, he has painted the figure of the Goddess of Liberty, reclining upon the back of America's eagle, with the following legend beneath: – "We're little, but some! You bet.' This is the facetious Gus's rendering of the motto of the Union – 'E Pluribus," etc. We have no doubt that many will be induced to follow the example of Tommy Dodds, and engage the services of one who can make of dingy bar walls and bar parlors 'Things of beauty and joys for ever.'"

Both Pierce and Gill stayed on at Hill End till the bust in 1874, then goes on the road again taking *A Mirror of Life* through difficult Austral terrain, and Pierce moves south through Wagga Wagga, Geelong and Echuca, where he painted the interior of the Steampacket Hotel in Echuca. *The Riverina Herald* of 27 January 1876 wrote the following: *Hotel Decoration: Lovers of art will be rewarded by visiting Mr. J. Bauld's Steampacket Hotel, its enterprising proprietor having converted it into a most attractive pictorial exhibition. It is ornamented on all sides with handsome paintings, all of an eminently Australian type, and executed in the highest order of the artistic excellence and taste. Prominent among the pictures is a beautifully executed sign of the house fronting the bar, comprising a view of a symmetrical and handsome river steamer of magnificent proportions under full steam on the Murray, towing a barge, loaded to overflowing with a cargo of wool – the scene depicting the Riverina trade in the height of its prosperity. This, the centrepiece, is surrounded on all sides with smaller meritorious illustration, the whole being delicately tined and giving the room a light and airy appearance most suitable for our hot climate. Mr. Bauld is to be congratulated upon his enterprise which will doubtless bring a highly increased patronage. The well-known local artist, Mr. Gus Pierce has designed and executed the whole of the paintings, which do him the greatest credit.*

Sadly, the building caught fire a few years later and the pictures were destroyed. *The South Australia Register* (13 September 1877) noted Batchelder's own benefit taking place at White's Rooms: *... the panoscopic scenes being of themselves excellent... Captain Gus Pierce, styled the 'Murray circumnavigator and flatboard commodore" will make his first appearance*. At his farewell dinner in Echuca he said "I am pleased to say I came here with nothing and I am leaving owing thousands of pounds". This bought the house down.

He completed a new *Mirror of Australia* panorama launched in 1879. These panoramas were toured to Geelong and Castlemaine – where he added to his troupe the male impersonator, Ellen Tremayne (De Lacy Evans) in 1881. The panorama was then shown in England.

In 1883 he acquired the Black Bull Hotel which he painted entirely, with the a Geelong paper noting: "Overlooking the entrance to the bar there is to be a painting 16 feet by 5 feet, giving a view of winter sports in Geelong, the subject being a football match on the Corio cricket ground "

With Geelong as his base for over a decade, and both of his sons settle in the district, several of his paintings have survived from this period. He also revisited the stage. As it happened, Pierce's partner at Hill End, William B Gill, had been performing in America, and wrote *Adonis* – In 1884, it became the first Broadway musical to play more than 500 straight performances.

In 1891 Pierce found work as an artist in Melourne, and acquired the Rose of Australia hotel, leaving Geelong the following year. Living as an artist in Peel Street, his wife Agnes acquired a new Colonial Wine Licence in 1893, but died the following year. Pierce left Australia in 1895 from Sydney to Vancouver.

Pierce died in 1920, and Yale University published *Knocking About* in 1924, prompting some interesting local reminicences. Old Warrior responded to a review in the *Sydney Morning Herald* (18 March 1925): *Gus Pierce was indeed, as you say, a "very versatile person." In 1867 I had occasion to ship some wool from Corowa on the Murray. I went on board a little river steamer to interview the captain, as to taking my wool. As I entered the cabin, the captain, who happened to be Captain Gus. Pierce, was sitting sideways on the table, writing a letter upside down, and with his left hand. The letter, it turned out, was one on business to the owners of the steamer. I wish I could write as legibly as it was written. Mind you, this letter was started at the bottom of the page and written backwards, and with the left hand. I was told afterwards that Pierce could write two letters simultaneously, one with each hand. I was incredulous, but several persons assured me they had seen him do it.*

The same afternoon I went into a little private room in Camillo Plains Hotel, Wahgunyah, just opposite Corowa. There were half a dozen people in the room. I sat down right beside Gus. Pierce. Someone said: "Gus, show us some tricks will you?" "What." he said, "with you fellows sitting right on top of me—and unprepared?" "Oh, yes," the other said. "It's up to you—wire in." Pierce asked for a hat, and putting it on the table said: "Have a look at what's in it." Forthwith he extracted potatoes, carrots, parsnips, etc., enough to fill a good-sized case. I was right up against him, and couldn't see how he did it.

Two days later 'Another Old Warrior', also responded:

The last time I heard of Captain Gus Pierce was that he had gone back to Boston, his birth place. His father was a ship-owner or builder, and I have read many letters from his sister, asking hint to return to Boston. I remember seeing him write a letter with his right hand, and answer it with his left simultaneously). Innumerable tricks with cards, and he was the best raconteur I ever heard.

And so we have these Tall Tales - All True by "our" Great America Delineator!

Tom Thompson

Before...

KNOCKING ABOUT

... After

1

I was born in West Medford, Massachusetts, in 1840, when that village was a little country community with all the usual characteristics of such places, and there my boyhood days were spent. From my mother's long line of sturdy seafaring forebears I inherited a strong love for the sea and for the adventures promised by life afloat. This love was increased by an extensive reading of books of travel, which so stimulated my desire to visit distant lands that, like many other youths of my time, I decided to become a sailor. My parents were greatly opposed to my plans, but finally became convinced of the strength of my determination; and, fearing that, if they indefinitely withheld their consent, I would run away without it, they decided to place me on a good ship, hoping that a three years' voyage would cure my wanderlust and that I would be glad to settle down a contented landsman. Accordingly I shipped before the mast on the *Oriental*, owned by Bacon & Company and commanded by Captain Osgood, bound for a three years' trading cruise in the China Seas. We sailed from New York Harbor in the middle of September of 1859.

The life aboard ship, the treatment of the crew, and the experiences of the voyage were those common to the merchant ships of the period, and I will not go into detail about these matters save to mention one incident, trivial enough in itself, yet of sufficient consequence to change the whole course of my life. The ship being short of provisions, the men were fed on the coarsest food. What resulted was a general petty thieving by the crew from the various provisions in the hold. This being discovered, two trustworthy men, of whom I was one, were detailed to go below whenever it was necessary to get any provender desired in the galley. From my earliest recollection I had always been afflicted with the disease known as a sweet tooth; and the constant sight of the molasses barrels offered by my journeys at the cook's command finally proved too much for me, and one day I fell to the extent of extracting a few ounces of this sticky sweetness. As is so often the fate of wrongdoers, I was discovered during my first attempt, and by the mate. Determined to cure me of this failing for sugar, Mr. Ballard forced me to drink a quart measure of the stuff even insisting that I thoroughly clean out the can in which it was placed. The result can readily be imagined: while thoroughly cured of all desire for molasses, I was a very sick young man. The mate's procedure soon reached the ears of the captain, who was so indignant that he reprimanded the mate in no very mild terms. This did not tend to make life any easier for me; for Ballard's attitude toward me increased so in brutality and malevolence that it finally became unbearable and was the direct cause of my abandoning the sea for a career which I had never even contemplated.

After a long and tedious voyage of some hundred days, the ship, after passing through many acres of squid in the old feeding grounds of the sperm whales, passed Port Phillip's Heads and came to anchor in Melbourne Bay, where she began discharging her cargo by lighters, as her draught was too great to allow her to lie alongside the quay. The studied cruelty of the mate, which was constantly increasing, and the foul and leaky condition of the ship, together with the wonder-tales of the great fortunes to be had in the gold fields, made the thought of desertion so sweet to me that I regarded the consequences of detection and capture as nothing compared with the pleasures of success. I watched keenly for any opportunity that would make escape even probable.

My appointment as coxswain of the captain's gig seemed to provide such a possibility. I dressed myself in all my clothes, putting one suit over the other, so as to be fully prepared when the chance came. But my bulky appearance aroused the suspicions of Ballard; and my hopes were temporarily shattered by my being put to hard work on the decks. I soon discovered, however, that I was not alone in my desire; for many of the men, either suffering from the gold fever or desiring to reship under better conditions (able seamen being then at a premium at Melbourne, where twenty or even thirty pounds was offered for a trip to London) jumped into bumboats and hastened to shore. I formed a conspiracy with three others, and we decided that at the first opportunity we would escape during the middle watch.

Shortly afterward occasion seemed to favor us. Of the lighters which were taking our cargo, one lay moored alongside. Another lay a few yards ahead with a small dinghy fastened at her stem. It was decided that one man should swim out, steal the dinghy, and return with it for the others. This was a most perilous undertaking, for the bay was full of sharks; their large dorsal fins could be plainly seen rushing swiftly through the water. We cast lots, sailor fashion, by twirling a knife in the circle. But the man selected, when about to dive off the anchor, turned coward at the sight of the ominous fins and returned. As even the chance of becoming a meal to one of these sharks seemed better to me than to remain longer as the object of Ballard's wrath and spleen, I volunteered to make the attempt. Retaining only my drawers and with my knife lanyard about my neck, I plunged in. I succeeded in reaching the dinghy, which I immediately detached; but, having no oars or other means of propulsion or guidance, I was rapidly drifted right under the counter stern of the *Oriental.* To escape detection I was obliged to go overboard again; and so, clinging to the gunwale and keeping under the bilge, I was dragged alongside until the boat was secured. This having satisfied the mate he soon disappeared, whereupon my companions came tumbling into the dinghy, bag and baggage. As an oar was absolutely necessary, I again went over and, swimming to the lighter moored to the ship, crossed her and soon gained the deck. There I was fortunate enough to find an oar lying, which I immediately pitched over into the boat. Just as I did so I caught sight of the mate; and, fearing detection, I had to move slowly and use much caution in retracing my way across the lighter. This caused some delay. Having accomplished it safely, I plunged in once more and swam for the dinghy. But the moon, suddenly rising, showed her far away—my cowardly companions, in their haste to get clear, having sculled off with all speed and left me alone in the shark- infested bay.To go back and acknowledge attempted desertion meant fearful punishment. To attempt to reach shore might mean anything; but I quickly decided to chance it, and struck out for my mile swim, making directly for the factory of the Sandridge

Sugar Refinery, which stood out strongly in the moonlight and made an excellent beacon. It was a very warm night, and, the current being favorable, I made excellent progress, resting for some time on a mooring buoy about half-way across. But during the remainder of the journey there set in the reaction from the excitement of my escape and from my anger at the desertion of my companions; and while still some distance from the shore, which to my weary eyes seemed to be constantly receding, I became exhausted and, giving up all hope, prepared to meet my fate—only to find myself on a sandbar in about three feet of water! This unexpected good fortune entirely revived my courage. After a short rest I again struck out for shore and, after a hard swim, landed safely on Saint Kilda beach at Emerald Hill just as day was breaking.

Emerald Hill was then merely a flat pasture abounding with thistle and bearing a few huts known as "wattle-and-daubs," from one of which a man was just emerging. I told him of my predicament and asked his assistance. He proved to be a kind-hearted, good-natured German, who, after giving me a good meal and dressing me in a red shirt and a pair of undersized moleskin trousers, advised me to give myself up and return to the ship. This was the last thing I intended to do, however, and, seeing that I was determined not to follow his advice, he finally referred me to a certain Charlie Brown who kept a sailors' boardinghouse in Melbourne. Then, giving me a penny to pay my passage on the ferry-boat across the Yarra, he wished me "Good luck!"

As I walked down the narrow plank walk to the primitive ferry, I took my last look at the *Oriental*—which, by the way, was never to return to the United States, for she was condemned at Java and her crew shipped home.

2

I FOUND Charlie Brown without difficulty; and at his place I also found my deserting shipmates. They offered profuse and elaborate excuses for their conduct toward me, but I paid no heed to them and was much gratified to learn later that they all got drunk, were arrested, put in the hulks, and returned to the ship, where they served without pay until released at Java.

Brown gave me a suit of large checked plaid and a pair of shoes from some indebted Scotchman's kit; and, having cut my long hair, he offered me a job. A certain Colonel Robinson, who was about to sail for Calcutta with a cargo of horses for the British Army, wanted hostlers. He offered four pounds a month, one pound in advance. Although I preferred to remain on land for a while, this seemed big pay to me, and I accepted. But that afternoon while walking in the Fitzroy Garden I fell in with a fellow countryman, Jonathan Minot of Boston, who had just been discharged from the bark *Pepper* and whose head was full of the wonderful opportunities offered in the gold fields. He finally induced me to abandon my prospective trip to India and accompany him to Bendigo. Thinking it wiser not to return to the whereabouts of Brown or Robinson, I immediately started on the road while Minot returned to his lodging at McLeod's "Corkscrew Inn" to get together his belongings. That night, after an eight-hour walk of some twenty miles, I slept in a deserted hut at Bald Hill; and there I was overtaken the next morning by Minot, who had been lucky enough to get a ride up on a dray. We immediately started on and walked to Gisborne, where we saw on a gate-post a notice: "WANTED. Two men to grub." Not knowing just what "grub" meant and thinking that it might refer to some kind of food, we decided to apply, for we were both very hungry. Accordingly we found ourselves hired to grub gum trees at two shillings a tree. This work consisted in digging around the tree and uncovering the roots, which were then cut away so as to expose the large tap root. That night we slept in a shack with some six others, on beds made of meal sacks and inhabited by some very lively little insects. The next morning we were led out to a large gum tree some four feet in diameter and set to work with pick and shovel. After working hard and steadily all day we had only succeeded in uncovering the roots; and as this seemed anything but a profitable employment for two prospective fortune-makers, we decided to take Scotch leave.

Just as we were going through the gate, our employer came out of the shack. In lighting his pipe behind a haystack, he set fire to it. At the same time a man on horseback appeared at the gate, who proved to be the proprietor; and the incendiary, who was his cook, immediately accused us of the arson and implied that we were a bad pair anyway. We were thereupon removed to the Gisborne police station, where we were fed by the policeman's wife and restrained until night, when we were marched to Castlemaine to be tried for arson—then a capital offense!

However, our general appearance of honesty and the straightforwardness of our story in opposition to the charge of our accuser, who proved to be a "cockatoo farmer" out for penal servitude, won us our acquittal; and our impecunious condition resulted in the subscription of a purse of ten pounds, which good fortune was further enhanced by the fact that the manager of the Castlemaine stables of Cobb & Company, owners of the coach line, proved to be an American. He became interested in us to the extent of placing Minot in charge of the way-stable at Ravenswood at three pounds a week and employing me there as a hostler at one third that wage.

While we were employed there a certain government official offered me what appeared to be a better position. This was a Mr. James Thomlow Smith, Assistant Surveyor. At that time it was customary for the government to allow persons holding this position sixty pounds perannum for two servants, who must be man and wife. Mr. Smith, having had considerable difficulty in procuring and retaining married couples, determined to try single persons. He requested me to sign articles for myself and wife, agreeing to find me a mate. I was soon at work as a general chore man, and a buxom young woman was found by my master to act as cook and to be officially known as Mrs. Pierce.

I soon wearied of this variety of matrimony, which was constantly leading to numerous complications, and parted from my nominal spouse without regret to become a clerk in McLeod's General Store at Swankey Flat, where I worked for several weeks. I then entered, as a common navvy or laborer, the employ of a small contracting firm known as Duxbury & Jackson, which was building the Big Hill Tunnel for the Melbourne & Bendigo Railroad. My clerical ability raised me in a few days to the position of time-keeper, and I was established at the wicker gate to time the navvies, with explicit orders to dock any man ten minutes late a quarter of a day's pay. My position was not, as can readily be believed, very popular with the men. In fact, a short time afterward Bronson, the government time-keeper, was murdered by O'Neil and I was given his position. But my roving nature and my desire to get to the gold fields would not allow me to hold it long. I threw up my billet, determined to strike out for the diggings. But fate intervened in the form of a certain Mezzetti, overseer of the Fenton Brothers' Ravenswood cattle ranch, who employed me to herd a flock of two hundred scabby sheep.

Often on the sheep ranches some of the animals become infected with a kind of eczema which causes scabs to form all over the skin and the wool to drop off. As this disease of the flocks and herded separately. I was instructed in my duties, given a week's rations (they consisted of two pounds of brown sugar, half a pound of tea, six pounds of flour, half a pound of the tobacco known as Barrett's Twist, and a tin of salt and pepper), and, accompanied by a collie sheep dog, sent out to watch the diseased flock. It was located in a little valley of kangaroo grass, where the sheep were feeding on sage and salt brush. Here I erected a *mia-mia,* which consists of a pole placed horizontally between two trees with long dried strips of bark from the red gum or eucalyptus tree resting against it. These slabs are shifted from one side of the pole to the other in accordance with the direction from which the wind is blowing. Here I was ordered to remain to prevent the sheep from straying back into the flocks and to protect them from the dingoes or warrigals, native dogs very similar to wolves.

All went well for a few days. The collie kept the sheep rounded up during the day and drove them into the low two-foot bough-built hurdles at night. I occupied my nights by killing the vicious bulldog ants and shooting the innumerable possums which abounded in that region. My days were employed in curing the skins of the possums in the native fashion (which is simply to peg them down on the ground and cover them with salt and ashes) and in reading two books which I had got hold of—one of which, Collins's *Woman in White,* caused my downfall. One day, wholly immersed in this story, I became quite oblivious of my surroundings, and my flock vanished. Waking to this realization, I searched for them in vain. I crossed the lonely grave at Dead Man's Gully and returned to the station. There Mezzetti, after a round scolding, discharged me without wages; and again I set my face toward Bendigo.

3

MY last employment not having been remunerative, I went on foot, stopping as seemed advisable to rest. At Kangaroo Flat I dined at Gunn's "Glasgow Arms," off the same old gumwood table and in the same little low-studded room used by the celebrated Lola Montez when that love of a Bavarian monarch made her Australian tour two years before.

On my arrival at Bendigo I immediately got employment in John Ely's bowling alley and shooting gallery, under the old Lyceum Theatre. This establishment was well advertised by an old cockatoo attached to a fruit stand, which used to cry "*Bendigo Advertiser*" in a shrill voice and then sell that paper, holding out his claw for the penny, which he then threw into a can fastened to his perch, to the great delight of the Saturday night crowd of miners. The miners generally came to town on that night to cash their bags of gold at the bank and make things gay. Their usual costume was rather flashy—white moleskin trousers with red sashes in which were stuck their pistols— and they always attracted attention. They frequented a popular oyster house kept by Jim Clegg, born and bred on Copp's Hill, Boston.

I soon learned that all the available mining ground at Bendigo was already claimed and being worked, and that, if I wished to mine, I must go elsewhere; so, together with three other young fellows, I walked on to the new fields at New Inglewood, some thirty miles north.

All was bustle and excitement at the time when we arrived at this raw new town of something less than a thousand inhabitants. We took lodgings at the United States Hotel, kept by Moody, Kennedy & McCann. Since we had not money enough to work a claim, employment was necessary; and I again went to work for Cobb & Company at their stable, then managed by Frank Mansfield, a native of Stoneham, Massachusetts, for three pounds a week. At the same time I washed dishes and blacked boots at the hotel for my board.

One day at Mansfield's request, being clever at lettering, I painted for the stable a small sign prohibiting smoking. It was hardly dry before the colored proprietor of the Dunolly Hotel saw it and asked me to make a large canvas sign for his house. I set to work with hammer, nails, paint, and brush, producing a twenty-six-foot creation three feet high, bearing "Dunolly Hotel" in two-foot black letters. More orders resulted; and the new sign-painter was in such demand that he found no time to devote to harness cleaning. So, with Mansfield's best wishes, I left the stable and gave myself to supplying New Inglewood with various styles of signs. But after the original demand was supplied, business slackened, and I was forced to look for other employment. I was hired by George Milbanks the butcher, for two hours daily, to sell Milton and Marlborough meat pies from a tin heater before his shop. In this I was very successful, for I resorted to all sorts of tricks and monkeyshines to attract custom, calling into play what powers of ventriloquism and legerdemain I had practiced as a boy.

Milbanks's next neighbor was a Greek doctor named Kanidyotti, who had a man-servant called Antonio. The doctor owned a large, handsome kangaroo dog which was a great nuisance to the butcher, owing to his cleverness in stealing meat. Milbanks complained of this at numerous times without avail; and one day when the animal was mysteriously poisoned, suspicion fastened itself upon the butcher. Early one morning as I was carrying two full pails of water from the waterhole to the house, I passed the stable of the Greek. Antonio, who sat in the doorway cleaning a bridle, began to taunt me and accuse me of having killed the dog, following his uncomplimentary remarks by throwing stones at me. I retaliated and began to stone him in return, whereupon he drew a pistol and fired at me. The bullet missed me, but, striking a rock, ricocheted and, passing through my hat and scalp, flattened out on my skull. I dropped unconscious and, falling on the buckets, overturned them, and the blood from my wound rapidly colored the water, giving me a very gory appearance. Paddy Belfield, an Irish actor living opposite, heard the shot and in his excitement rushed out in only his shirt, forgetting to put on his drawers, which he carried in his hand—an episode which naturally gave a comic turn to the accident and later caused Belfield much discomfiture. I soon regained consciousness and was immediately taken to the police camp, where Dr. Redcliffe dressed my wounds and Detective Slattery questioned me regarding the assault. Dr. Kanidyotti soon appeared, very much frightened and offering all sorts of inducements to stop proceedings, but his overtures were refused. The police hunted diligently for Antonio for months without discovering any trace of him. Many years later he was arrested for vagrancy in Sydney, and that same night died in jail of heart disease.

Having remained some time with Milbanks and saved some money, I blocked out and took up a mining claim together with my friends from Bendigo, who had also managed to accumulate a few pounds. It was beside the Pretty Sally, one of the richest in the diggings. We worked hard at it for many weeks, until, having used up all our money and our credit too, we were forced to abandon it and also vacate our comfortable lodgings at the "Old Folks at Home," a hotel kept by Joe Kitchen, the celebrated pugilist who for many years held the championship gold belt for heavyweights.

Broke and in debt, I returned to the friendly Mansfield, who put me in temporary charge of the coach way-stable at White Flag, a little village consisting of a blacksmith's shop and a couple of prospectors' huts half way between Tarrengower (now called Maldon) and Hammond's Poverty Claim, one of the richest in the district. About a week later the permanent keeper arrived, and I was again jobless. But, wishing to send an old white horse called Napoleon to the coach stable at Tarrengower, he suggested that I ride it there and see what I could find in that town.

Accordingly, about dusk I started off along the narrow bush road. I was soon overtaken by a violent electric storm, during which I dismounted near a little sluggish creek and got under cover among the bushes. While I was there, two rough looking fellows appeared suddenly, knocked me down, and rode off on the emperor's namesake. When I recovered from my surprise and picked myself up, soaked and dazed, a flash of dazzling lightning revealed to my startled eyes the figure of a man hanging from a gibbet directly in front of me. This was too much for my nerves. Fleeing from the horrid sight, I rushed into the creek, now transformed into a torrent, waded across in the pitchy darkness, up to my armpits in water, and hastened with all the expedition possible to Tarrengower, where I fell, more dead than alive, into Teddy Ellis's "Kangaroo Arms" and told my story. I was informed that the thieves had brought the horse to the coach stable and turned him over to the owners, having evidently desired only to use him as a means of conveyance, without further intention of larceny. My mention of the hanging man seemed to fill the occupants of the room with uncontrollable mirth, and they set up a howl of laughter. Sometime previously, it seemed, a dead woman had been discovered under an overturned wagon at Mother Molloy's Creek. Her husband had been suspected of the crime, for which he had been tried and executed. Some gruesome wit had carved the figure of a hanging man on the bark of a large gum tree near the spot of the murder, and it was this apparition that had frightened me.

Attached to Ellis's hotel was a concert room where large audiences of miners were delighted nightly by the performances of the Morgan Brothers, harpists, and Dave White, expert on the banjo, guitar, and mandolin. As from early boyhood I had been much given to singing, dancing, hanky-panky stunts, and the like, I felt that my powers of entertainment might be turned to some profit. Having shown what I could do, I was offered the chance to take the boards for half an hour nightly, while my days were to be occupied in sawing wood and doing other chores, all for the magnificent sum of thirty shillings and board. Not having a particularly critical audience, I made quite a success in my vaudeville act, receiving very gratifying applause for my rendering of *Joe Bowers, Betsey Baker,* and *Drunk Again.* Thinking my value much increased by this success, I declined to saw wood, turned my attention to stage carpentry and painting, and produced a couple of pieces of scenery representing a garden and an interior, for which I was enriched by an extra three pounds.

Having furnished Ellis with all the settings he thought he required, I moved on to Dunolly, which had just emerged from a primitive diggings into an established town of substantial frame buildings. Acting and scenepainting were unfortunately in no demand here; so I was obliged to do what I could for self-support. I managed to make a living by painting a few little pictures and assisting Frank Weston, an Alabama man, in hawking his famous "Wizard Oil," which was supposed to be a panacea for every ill known to human flesh. It was here that I formed my acquaintanceship with the famous Julius Vogel, who eventually became Sir Julius and was so prominent for his governmental experiments and reforms in New Zealand in the seventies. He was then the editor of the *Maryborough and Dunolly Times*. Being very fond of billiards, we spent almost every evening together enjoying the game at old Peter Frame's hotel.

About midwinter (June), having tired of Dunolly and seeing no very encouraging prospects there, I decided to try Melbourne. I arrived there almost penniless, but was lucky enough to meet a Canadian named William Chisholm, who engaged me to paint a picture of the great American falls for his Niagara Hotel. I had not seen the falls, never having been out of Massachusetts before my sailing on the *Oriental*, and I did not remember ever having seen a picture of them; but as Chisholm's patrons were in the same boat, the view which I managed to produce was very satisfactory, and old Chisholm, when questioned, would lean across the bar and murmur, "Perfect picture, fellows; almost makes me homesick to look at it!"

At this time Harvey & Maxey, who had been touring the country with their American company of San Francisco Minstrels, disbanded, and Paul Maxey "from the Pacific slope" was billed at Deane's Royal Charter Concert Room. As he was a regular patron of Chisholm, I often met him there and managed to impress him with the idea that I could be of assistance in some of his acts; with the result that he engaged me to take part in the little minstrel sketch which he was producing. But after a few weeks of this work my uneasy nature again asserted itself; and, as I had formerly had some experience in photographic work with Lay & Hayward of Boston, I entered the studio of Batchelder & O'Neil, two Salem men who afterward became the foremost of Australian photographers. I worked for some weeks at their Melbourne studio under the supervision of Johnson, who later returned to his home in California to gain fame as a landscape painter; and I was then sent to Bendigo to a little branch studio run by the younger brother of the senior-partner, Benjamin Batchelder.

My days were occupied, but my evenings were my own; and, still attracted by the gleam of the footlights, I sought and gained employment at the Lyceum Theatre, where my evenings were spent in helping the property man at a pound a week. The scenic artist, John Fry, observing that I had some ability with brush and pencil, offered to instruct me in scene-painting. This work proved so attractive that my photographic duties were rather neglected, and Batchelder finally advised me to "move over to the theatre for good," which advice I immediately followed, becoming general utility man, scene-painter, and carpenter, assisting the property man and playing minor roles in James Nathan's Lyceum Stock Company.

My progress and improvement in scene-painting was so marked that when the celebrated Houson Family of opera singers opened its season with *Norma*, I was allowed to produce the entire Stonehenge scene unaided. The elder Houson, on examining this scene, was much pleased with it, although in showing it the gear gave way and the roller jumped from its socket and bowled over the star, to his great discomfiture and the amusement of some of the other members of his "family."

The Housons were followed by Marsh's Juvenile Troupe, an American company of children who played a short engagement of high-class drama and Shakespeare.

They were succeeded by the great American actor of the time. Joseph Jefferson arrived at Bendigo in 1862, supported by the Melbourne Royal Stock Company, which included such eminent artists as John Dunn, Rogers, Julia Matthews, Richard Stuart, the Steeles, and the Melvilles—an exceedingly strong company and hard to equal. Mr. Jefferson opened with *Our American Cousin*, making a great success. But the papers, while complimenting the star on his ability to portray American characters, rather doubted his capacity for English drama; whereupon the great artist took up the challenge and won immense applause in his rendering of Bob Acres in *The Rivals*, and also in other English comedy parts, his inimitable portrayal being so superior to anything that had ever been shown in the country that all criticism was suffocated.

As I had acquitted myself with credit in some little roles in the Jefferson productions, I was now considered as a regular member of the Lyceum company. I went with it to Castlemaine, a diggings of some repute about twenty-three miles from Bendigo, then famous as the home of the celebratedexplorer Robert O'Hara. After a few weeks' engagement at the Royal Theatre, kept by Frank Beddard (also proprietor of the well-known "House of Blazes," a rough dance hall), I decided to return to Melbourne to see what it might have for me.

Fortune appeared in the form of a certain George Hooper, an American vendor of patent medicines who then controlled an alleviator of all ills, which panacea he called by a long and guttural Indian name, and of which the main ingredient was essence of peppermint. We formed a partnership, and I started out to introduce this wonderful cure-all throughout the country. My coming was heralded by a profuse scattering of advance posters bearing this inscription:

WILL APPEAR TONIGHT.

Gus B. Pierce, the great American Delineator and Serio-Comic Lecturer —Presenting Hooper and Peirce's celebrated alleviator, an instant cure for all pains. External, Internal, and Eternal !

Entertainment Gratis.

Being so well advertised, my appearance upon the scene with a pair of horses, light wagon, good clothes, and a banjo was calculated to impress the audience. My first appearance at Castlemaine was to a crowded house.

But after the entertainment was finished and the sale of medicine began, the audience rapidly diminished, until in disgust I turned out the lights and went. This was only a forerunner of the successive performances. The scheme was an entire failure. And when I turned my attention to getting orders from the druggists and shopkeepers, they refused, stating that they were already overstocked with Weston's Wizard Oil which I had sold them, and which they never expected to get rid of! Unable to meet expenses, I sold the outfit, dissolved partnership, and returned again to Melbourne.

The Maori war then being in progress in New Zealand, quantities of supplies were constantly being shipped there provisions and many adventurous spirits anxious to carve a fortune in the New Zealand gold fields, of which fabulous stories were then in circulation. Finding nothing there of interest or promise, I remained with the steamer and returned to Australia, leaving her at Sydney, whence I worked my passage to Melbourne on the old *You-Yangs*, one of the earliest steam coasters of the pioneer firm of Howard Smith & Sons.

4

AT this time I made the acquaintance of a Mr. Hughes, of the firm of Hughes, Gouge & Putnam, butchers having slaughter-houses at X Creek and Bullock Creek. Mr. Hughes invited me to his house at the former place for a few days. On the first evening after dinner I endeavored to entertain the company with various sleight-of-hand tricks, during which performance the servants were allowed in. One of them, a large Irish girl, green and of slight mental capacity, was much frightened by what struck her simple mind as my supernatural powers. She was constantly exclaiming in a loud whisper, "Sure, the divil's in the man!" This attracted the attention of Mrs. Hughes, who said in fun: "Bridget, Mr. Pierce is a remarkable man. Now, if he chose, though of course he would not do it, he could enter your room to-night, no matter how many bolts or locks fastened the door and window." The timid servant said nothing, but she looked much alarmed and avoided me as much as possible during the rest of the evening.

When the family had retired, Mr. Hughes took me aside and suggested that it would be a good joke to make his wife's words come true. So, before Bridget got upstairs, he showed me a ladder resting against the servant's window. I mounted it and, having gained the room, threw it over to the ground and hid myself behind the bed. The girl having got into bed, I moved to the door and knocked. "Go away, you can't git in!" shrieked the frightened maid. Jumping into the middle of the moonlit room, with hand on breast in the posture of Mephisto in *Faust,* I thundered "I am here!" The girl gave one yell and fainted. More frightened now than the girl herself, I routed up the household, and after some time and trouble

Bridget was herself again. But somehow the joke was less amusing than Mr. Hughes had anticipated.

Two days later I accompanied Mr. Putnam to Bullock Creek, where I was employed to drive a meat wagon about the place and to Queen's Head. There were some twenty regular customers scattered along the different bush roads. Shortly after our arrival, Mr. Putnam was obliged to go away, and affairs were placed in my hands. I was given a bottle of poison and instructed to saturate some meat and leave it about the premises for a trio of kangaroo dogs which were constantly visiting the place and chewing the scrags and shoulders of the slaughtered cattle, which were hung by the heels on the gallows about the hut. I was also cautioned to watch Peter, a queer-looking pock-marked old lag who acted as cook,—he had a peculiar mode of hair dressing, always wearing two long corkscrew curls in front of his ears,—and see that he did not get drunk, as he usually did whenever Mr. Putnam was absent.

The first night of my command was a very clear moonlit one. The poisoned meat lay temptingly exposed on the ground while I, in hiding, awaited results with the eager anticipation of a Borgia. Before long the dogs appeared. They were large and strong, these hunters of the kangaroo, being crossed between a greyhound and a stag hound, receiving swiftness from the former and power from the latter. Without compunction they attacked the prepared meat. They ate it with gusto, whisked their tails, leaped the fence, and vanished unharmed. This was beyond my comprehension; so I went to call Peter, but found with dismay that he had taken Dutch leave. However, thinking that I had not used a sufficient amount of poison, the following night I doubled the dose, but with the same result. Once more I tried it, only to receive a third disappointment. On the following morning both Putnam and Peter arrived at the same time, the latter plainly showing the marks of his three days' dissipation. He made a rush for the poison bottle and, finding it empty, moaned, "My salts! where are my salts?" "Why, man," I exclaimed, "what do you mean? Isn't that poison?" "No," replied the inebriated cook, "them was my salts. I marked 'em p'ison so's they'd be left alone!" Which statement readily accounted for the continuation of dog life in the vicinity after the consumption of nearly a whole ox of presumably poisoned meat.

Three weeks of meat-cart driving was sufficient for me. I left it and went to work for the pound-keeper, a certain English gentleman named Gower, who shortly after inherited a fortune and gave up the position. After some weeks of copying the brands of stray cattle in the pound book, I wearied of this, decided to return to photography, and again entered the employ of Batchelder & O'Neil, who again sent me to Bendigo. The firm was then under contract to supply a quantity of Australian scenes for an exposition shortly to be held at London. With another man I was sent on a photographic expedition. We were furnished with a little black push-cart holding the camera and other necessaries, and we were to get pictures of all objects of interest. As the work was most disagreeable, owing to the intense heat and horrible dust, any opportunity for a change looked good to me, and I shortly found one. An amateur photographer, Joseph Creelman, who was greatly interested in aboriginal Australian life, desired an experienced man to accompany him on an artistic expedition into the native communities; and, being well recommended by Batchelder, I secured the position.

Creelman furnished excellent equipment for the work, and we were well supplied with all necessary articles, conveniently packed in a good strong wagon drawn by a pair of sturdy horses. We left Bendigo in January of 1863 and took up the old Burke and Wills trail for Castle Donnington, or Swan Hill, as it was commonly called, owing to the great numbers of black swans that congregated there.

Our first stop was at Serpentine River, where we entered a large camp of blacks. At first we were unable to make any photographs, owing to the natives' fear of the camera. The gins, as the females are called, set up a terrific howling whenever it was pointed in their direction, and the rumpus caused the appearance of the old king, who crawled out of his hut and approached us. His appearance was anything but regal: he was extremely filthy and clad only in an apron of small dimensions, and his sore eyes were covered with flies. Having some acquaintance with pidgin English, he opened the conversation with a protest: "King gabba all same white pellar! Bailem tinket you triem shotem gin! Black pellar no like you shotem gin!" We naturally denied any such intention and finally persuaded the old fellow to put his head under the focusing cloth and look through

the lens. He showed great delight at this experience, shouting joyfully, "Bailem tink gin all same like it stand on head!" Whereupon all the court and populace wanted to follow the king's example. After two or three had looked, Creelman decided to prevent further waste of time by capping the lens, upon which the disgusted black under the cloth observed: "All black lak night! All big moon no jump up!" As his majesty was now thoroughly satisfied with the innocence of our purpose, he scornfully remarked to his subjects, "All black pellars big and bloody pool!" and, lining up his court, he aided greatly in the procuring of some excellent negatives.

That night a corroboree was held in our honor, at which the entire male population appeared entirely nude, with their heads, ribs, and extremities striped with white pipe clay to resemble skeletons. Forming in line, each holding a little green bough, they began to dance slowly. Gradually they increased the speed until they reached a state of high excitement. Their movements were then of great rapidity as they jumped about, whirling in the air and waving the branches. At regular intervals they seemed to vanish altogether, for on turning their backs, which were free of pipe clay, they could not be distinguished from the surrounding darkness. All these movements were performed in perfect unison and rhythm to the monotonous beating of possum-skin drums made from rolled rugs. The beating was done with nulla-nullas (short sticks with knobs at the end) in the hands of the gins, who sat in a line at the feet of the dancers.

The following morning the natives aided us in fording the Serpentine and getting our supplies across in their canoes. These boats are of the most primitive construction, being nothing more than a large strip of bark cut to the correct size, with pointed ends, from the eucalyptus tree and dried in the sun, and shaped by a cross-stick in each end. The heat of the sun naturally curls the bark and produces a rude boat.

Having arrived safely on the other side, we bade our new friends farewell. After crossing the monotonous and barren Durham Ox Plain, following the well-beaten trail along the telegraph line, we arrived at Reedy Lake station, so named from a cluster of little lakes almost overgrown with reeds. This station was owned by Fenton Brothers, and the first person I saw was Mezzetti, the overseer, who was riding the trail with one of his boundary riders. I immediately hailed him and asked if he had found the scabby sheep which I lost at Ravenswood. He was much surprised to see me and invited us to the ranch homestead; but as it was off our route we declined and substituted a dinner at the local inn, where we had an excellent meal of kangaroo haunch and jugged hare.

During the afternoon a crowd of blacks appeared. While we were photographing them, one of the men accidentally knocked over and broke a bottle of acetic acid which was standing near the camera. Greatly distressed at the injury which he felt himself to have done us, and wishing to express his contrition for the deed and to endeavor to make amends for the injury, he pointed to the offending toe with which he had inadvertently kicked over the bottle, placed it on a stump, and, before we realized what he was about, severed it from his foot with one blow of his tomahawk. Creelman, who was greatly addicted to the habit of tobacco-chewing, hastily planked his quid on the bleeding stump, and Mezzetti, pulling from his pocket a bit of silk such as ranchmen use for the snappers of their long flexible whips, dressed the wound. He forgot the inordinate love of the blacks for the weed. Shortly afterward the patient was observed dragging his mutilated foot along the dusty road, contentedly and happily chewing the quid, his satisfied expression betraying no memory of his pain.

In the morning our horses, which had been placed in a small paddock belonging to Booth & Holloway, owners of the Durham Ox station and renowned for their excessive piety, were missing, and we were told they must have been stolen by bush-whackers! Although we had grave doubts of the truth of this statement, Creelman decided to waste no time in searching for them, but returned immediately to Bendigo and purchased a pair of gray mares from Cobb & Company. These he brought back the next day as leaders on the coach driven by the celebrated Bill Garden. This coach driver was an institution on the Swan Hill line, and many stories are told regarding his bravery and prowess. He was a Canadian of some six feet in height, large of bone and well supplied with muscle, and he always wore a luxuriant yellow beard which fell considerably below his waist. Creelman sold him the chance to recover the stolen horses for ten pounds, and Garden seemed to have no doubt of his being able to secure them.

A new start was made the following morning. While passing Lake Boga we enjoyed a new experience in fishing. The lake seemed literally covered with wild ducks, whose beating wings made a great noise on striking the water. We saw a fish-hawk plunge in and secure a perch, which he brought ashore. But before he could poke its eyes out Creelman bowled him over with a stone, and we had the prey for lunch.

The well-grassed plain about Lake Boga is remarkable for the size and number of its many salt pans. These are neither more nor less than ponds which have become perfectly dry during the hot season, the receding waters leaving a deep surface of pure white glistening salt, which, on refining, becomes an article of commerce in great demand in the sheep and cattle countries for the curing of hides. It is not adapted to culinary use, for which Liverpool salt is almost entirely employed. Tons of this plain salt are shipped down the Murray to Adelaide every season, and the procuring and refining constitute a flourishing industry, for the beds are inexhaustible, new strata of salt being formed every year.

We spent one night in bivouac on the shores of the lake. The following day we completed our journey to Swan Hill, where we put up at Raynes's Hotel. On approaching the settlement we observed in the distance a brick pillar some eight feet in height, on which appeared to be a group of figures. On a nearer view it proved to be the pedestal of the contemplated monument to Burke and Wills, this having been their last stopping place in Victoria before crossing the Murray into New South Wales to vanish into oblivion at Cooper's Creek. The ostensible statuary consisted of a trio of goats contentedly reposing on its cap. Swan Hill was then a comparatively primitive settlement, its only brick building being the new telegraph station.

My short association with Creelman terminated here, owing to an athletic contest. Though sorry to be unemployed again, I did not much regret losing this job; photographic work in those days was very tedious, with its long exposures and old collodion process.

On the afternoon of our arrival a large congregation of some two hundred blacks, who had come to the station for their annual allowance of supplies from the government stores, held an exhibition of their native games, at which a powerful and finely built fellar known as The Kangaroo proved himself the champion, distancing all his competitors in throwing the spear, twirling the boomerang, running, and jumping. In the last-named he covered forty feet in four consecutive jumps, amid the applause of the spectators. Now, I had always been inclined to athletics at home, and during my school days I had won the admiration of my mates by what I considered to be the remarkable accomplishment of a running jump over the slowly plodding horse of old Dr. Fuller as that worthy took his way down the main street of Medford. I began to talk with Creelman about jumping. He considered himself a great jumper; and we finally arranged for a match that evening in the hotel billiard room. During the contest, Creelman failed to jump over a handkerchief held about three feet from the floor between two men, which I had just grazed. He refused to acknowledge me as winner; a quarrel ensued, during which I was unlucky enough to knock him down; and I was immediately free to look for another occupation.

While waiting for something favorable to be offered, I spent a few days as a guest of Dr. Gummo, the resident physician in charge of a small hospital for victims of pleuropneumonia, a disease very common among shepherds and cattlemen because of their constant exposure to all phases of the weather. Dr. Gummo had another guest, a Mr. Shires, a man most remarkable for his ability to handle venomous snakes. He had compounded and was trying to introduce an antidote for snake bites, in which the physician was greatly interested. Shires, who was very tall and extremely thin, was remarkably quick of action and most dexterous in handling serpents. He seemed entirely devoid of fear of them.

On the first morning of my visit, our host and I accompanied Shires on a snake hunt. We were greatly interested to observe his methods of procedure. As all Australian snakes, with the exception of the beautifully marked carpet snake, are extremely venomous, it requires great skill and daring to attempt their capture alive; especially as, unless taken at bay or suddenly startled, they hastily retreat into their holes on the approach of man. It was Shires's custom to allow the snake to creep into a hole until only about five or six inches of its tail was visible, which he then grasped under his second finger and held tightly between the first and third, dragging the creature from the hole and quickly thrusting it into a close wire cage held in his left hand. This method required not only skill but strength, for the belly scales of the snake cling tenaciously to the floor of its burrow and offer considerable resistance.

Of course, nothing would satisfy me but to attempt to imitate Shires. It looked easy, and as a boy I had often caught the harmless little green snakes of New England and snapped off their jaws as one cracks a whip. Having observed the capture of a few reptiles, I decided to try my hand. I approached a disappearing tiger snake and, with much boldness mingled with fear, grasped the tail and began to pull. I was greatly startled to see the animal's head rapidly appearing, it having doubled on itself and returned to investigate the difficulty of its retreat. By a backward spring I was just able to evade a sudden and uncomfortable demise.

That evening in the hotel billiard room Shires gave an exhibition at which he demonstrated the unexampled powers of his antidote in the most conclusive manner, and procured numerous contracts to clear different farms and ranches of snakes. The billiard table was covered with a canvas sheet, and upon it was placed a large wire cage containing about forty reptiles—the ugly tiger snakes, the brown bodies of which are regularly marked with black stripes, the bellies slate-colored; the beautiful large black snakes, with their bright red bellies; and the small but dangerous death adders, in their mottled brown coats. Among the audience were two brothers named Pye, each of whom had only one eye, and who were inclined to be skeptical. They were butchers with an extensive business and owners of large droves of hogs which roamed at will over their numerous fields. The Pyes were much interested in the effect of snake bites on hogs, although they maintained that their animals were never bitten, but invariably exterminated the snakes. However, each had brought an experimental offering in the form of an antiquated rooster and a sucking pig.

Everything being in readiness, the porker was placed on the table. Shires opened the cage and, grasping the snake already selected by the victim's owner, shook it at the pig. The tiger sprang and fastened its fangs into its prey's fat jowls, where it hung about three seconds. Twenty seconds later the pig died in excruciating agony. While returning the reptile to the cage, Shires allowed it to bite him on his beardless chin, drawing considerable blood, which quickly coagulated. The audience was greatly alarmed, and Dr. Gummo begged to be allowed to cauterize the wound; but Shires refused and, taking a bottle of his antidote, which smelt strongly of ammonia, applied the solution to the wound with the cork. The bleeding ceased instantly, and the blood already drawn formed a small hard ball, which he snapped off with his fingers. Then, drinking a glass of whiskey, which he considered beneficial for poisons, he kept on the move, declaring that to remain quiet would be most conducive to dangerous results. This remarkable exhibition failed, however, to satisfy the skeptical Pyes, who declared that the snake had used all his poison on his first bite on the pig and therefore had nothing with which to inoculate Shires on the second bite. Whereupon the Australian St. Patrick offered further proof. The antiquated rooster was then placed on the table and another snake selected by one of the Pyes. To the horror of the spectators, Shires allowed this one immediately to bite him on the nose; then, after quickly applying the antidote, he shook the snake at the rooster, in which it sank its fangs. Two seconds later the herald of the dawn was no more. It was proved that the tiger snake is capable of poisoning at two consecutive attacks.

Twenty-two years later I met Shires again. He was then giving an exhibition of snake-charming at Frank Weston's Opera House, erected at Melbourne by the profits of the famous "Wizard Oil." He had failed to find any market for his antidote, owing to the skepticism which asserted that he was in some way snake-proof, and the public refused to purchase his remedy. During his Melbourne engagement Shires kept his snakes tightly caged in the conservatory of the hotel where he was stopping. One day Chief Drummond of the Melbourne police, entering the room, declared that fear of snakes was ridiculous and that to his belief no one had ever died of a snake bite. To show the courage of his convictions, he deliberately thrust his finger through the wire. It was bitten by a large tiger snake; and in a few minutes the chair of the Chief of Police was awaiting another occupant.

The *Lady Daly*.

Surveying the Murray River with Everest and our tracker.

5

MY first view of the Murray River, which forms the boundary between Victoria and New South Wales, made a great impression on me. It was a beautiful wide stream winding slowly through a vast treeless plain. Upon this plain fed numerous descendants of the camels deserted by the Burke and Wills expedition; they were running wild, and they gave the scene a decidedly Oriental aspect. I was strongly of the opinion that the river was navigable; and, learning that a line of steamboats had been established between Wentworth and Port Goolwa at the delta in Encounter Bay, some twelve hundred miles below, I determined to go down, get a position with the company, and study the navigation of the stream in order to become a river, pilot and explore the upper waters.

A few days later Mr. Macdonald, who owned the coach line between Swan Hill and Wentworth, hired me to drive two gentlemen to Kilnine, a sheep ranch some seventy miles down the river in New South Wales. This employment would give me transportation to within some twenty miles of my desired destination. We made an early start with a pair of horses and one of the famous Concord coaches built in New Hampshire, U.S.A., and imported at the exorbitant price of seventy pounds. We forded the river and moved eastward on the bush road, which runs on a high ridge between Snake Swamp and the river, the course of which it followed. The swamp seemed covered with legions of feathered creatures—thousands of ibex, white cranes, native companions, piebald geese, and Cape Java blue duck. They rose in myriads on our approach, their flapping wings making a thunderous noise. On the other side great quantities of gray wood duck covered the river. After a night's stop at Tyntynda station (owned by Peter Beveridge, one of the early pioneer ranchmen, whose brother had been murdered by visiting natives whom he was befriending some years before), I deposited my passengers at their destination, turned over the equipage to the Euston stable, and took the coach to Wentworth.

This town, although fairly large and important, owing to its position at the junction of the Darling and Murray rivers, which gave it some commercial importance as a port for the river boats, was retarded in its natural growth by the general attitude of its inhabitants, who were of Calvinistic origin, with narrow and prejudiced minds. In fact, their Puritanical attitude toward everything was a byword in the country. In one instance they even went so far as to force the resignation of an Inspector of Police because his wife, a very charming and attractive woman, was accustomed to sit in her window in a low-necked gown, playing with a young kitten which she allowed to lie upon her naked bosom!

While awaiting the arrival of the boat, I occupied my time as best I could with little odd jobs sufficient to support my self. Among other matters I painted a cart and emblazoned the royal arms of Britain on the barroom wall of a hotel kept by a passionately patriotic Englishman.

But my most interesting experience was as a bumbailiff for a Chinaman. The Douglas Family, a travelling troupe of vaudeville artists and acrobats, had been touring the region of the upper Darling and, after an unsuccessful trip, were bankrupt. As they were heavily indebted to John Egge, a Chinese storekeeper of whom they were also tenants, he procured a warrant against them and employed me, at half a sovereign per diem, to reside on the premises and make an inventory of the various goods and chattels in their possession, until such time as an auction could be held, by which the creditor hoped to regain part of the debt.

As the law provided that the bumbailiff must gain entrance between sunrise and sunset, amusing and trying incidents often occurred in connection with that functionary's gaining admittance. A story was then extant of a certain official who, having gained entrance to the house of a delinquent butcher, proudly boasted of his cleverness in effecting an entrance unobserved. "Are you positive that no one saw you come in'?" demanded the debtor, with an insinuating air of doubt as to the official's ability. "Certainly," replied the representative of the law; "I know my business, and none even suspect my presence here." Grabbing a large cleaver, the butcher rushed at him, roaring, "Then no one will ever see you come out!" These words and actions so frightened the astonished the butcher smiled complacently, bolted the doors, and took care that he should remain without.

However, I had no such difficulty. Being unknown to Mr. Douglas, I accomplished my purpose by a little diplomacy. The discovery of my business was taken most philosophically by the whole family—although, while taking the inventory, I was invited to step into the yard to count the poultry, which invitation I was wise enough to decline. The property listed showed very little of commercial value. It consisted largely of provisions and the various professional appurtenances of the troupe. As there was slight demand at Wentworth for papier-mache spears, Roman togas, ancient sandals, or pink tights, Mr. Egge seemed likely to realize but little from the sale. When the date arrived, the Douglas family, having con-sumed the provisions and secreted the best of their belongings, took to the road to Adelaide. After considerable excitement among the throng of expectant purchasers, the whole matter was looked at as a joke, and even Egge remarked, "Velly damned good pleased didn't bum house!" But he refused to pay me more than half of the agreed price, which was a total loss to him.

One morning the tedious waiting came to an end, and, with whistle screeching and gong ringing, the *Lady Daly*, a large American river boat with a tremendous stem wheel some twenty-four feet in diameter, arrived alongside her wharf and began discharging her cargo. She was typically American, having been built in Oregon and shipped in segments to Port Adelaide, where she was reassembled at Fletcher's yard. She was owned by the American firm of Murray & Jackson and manned mostly by American men. She flew a large American flag on her jackstaff, but her register was British, and she owed her name to the wife of the governor of Adelaide.

She had hardly been made fast before I was making my way up the gangplank, amidst her disembarking passengers, to the hurricane deck, where I asked a sailor if there was an American aboard. He referred me to the purser, who proved to be Arthur Lincoln Blake, a Bostonian who had attended the same private school in Medford that I had gone to, and who naturally became rather interested in me on that account. During our conversation I made some remark about drawing, and he asked me if I could make a chart of the river. The company was anxious to have one, and he would recommend me as a draughtsman if I thought I could do it. I instantly agreed to undertake the matter. Accordingly I accompanied

Mr. Blake on the return trip down the river to Goolwa, where the steamer went out of commission at Carson & Company's yards for repairs. From Goolwa we travelled by coach to Adelaide, passing through a most beautiful country, the fertile hills of which were covered with fine vineyards cultivated by the thrifty sons of Germany who had largely settled this region. After a few days at Adelaide we sailed for Melbourne in the steamer *Korong,* Captain William McLean, brother of Hell-fire Jack. Arriving after a pleasant trip of some seven hundred miles, we put up at the Globe Hotel, kept by the proprietors of the Golden Age at Tarrengower, where I had first taken to the boards. I was immediately recognized, and the time not occupied in business was agreeably spent among my old acquaintances.

Arrangements having been satisfactorily completed, I was engaged by Murray & Jackson to chart the Murray River from Albury to Goolwa. I was supplied with the necessary materials and instruments and sent to Echuca with a letter to Frederick Payne, the company's agent, on whom I was to draw for necessary expenses. Having gained what was necessary at Echuca, I passed through Wahgunyah to Albury and made preparations for fitting out my little expedition. I bought a strong fifteen-foot clinker-built boat provided with both sail and oars, in which I stowed only a limited amount of provisions, for I intended to get most of my supplies from the settlements and native camps along the shores. I hired a black boy for the heavy and dirty work and engaged the services of a versatile and entertaining dancing master named Everest as a cook and general assistant. Everything being in readiness, we pushed off bright and early one hot morning and began our long journey of some seventeen hundred and fifty miles down the river.

During this journey, which was undertaken during the hot dry season when the river was at its lowest level, I sat at a little table which I had rigged in the bow and not only surveyed and followed the course of the river, but took numerous soundings and plotted all obstructions, such as sawyers and snags. When any of these appeared particularly dangerous I would go ashore, select a tree in line with the obstruction, strip off a large piece of bark, and paint a red circle, lozenge, or star upon the trunk, marking the chart to correspond. Rough gauges were also placed on trees along the dangerous shallows, the depth being ascertained with a ten-foot sounding pole.

6

ON the first day's trip, which took us to Howlong, we found the river narrow and rapid, with many sand-spits off the points and the bights filled with huge snags. The banks were, in general, low and grassed; but there were occasional high and heavily wooded bluffs with widely separated clearings in which the various homesteads of the stations were situated. Howlong was then hardly worthy of the name of even a settlement: it consisted of little save a public house, general store, and blacksmith shop, and the hostelry had so little to offer in the way of entertainment that we preferred to camp on the river bank for the night, after our hot and tedious day.

The next day took us to Wahgunyah, at which point was erected the first bridge ever built across the Murray, connecting New South Wales with Victoria. Here we found quite a flourishing town, owing to the establishment a few years previously of some large steam flour mills by John Foord, or "King Foord," as he was more commonly called. From Wahgunyah we rowed on down the river past Brockalbry's station, owned by Gray & Neill, to Collondina, a large sheep station belonging to Robert Brown, a magistrate of huge dimensions. The weather was favorable to the survey, but the extreme heat was almost unbearable, and every night found us pretty well fagged out. It was my custom on making camp to review the day's work thoroughly and thus impress on my memory accurate pictures of the various portions of the river which were of more than common interest. These views seemed to be photographed on my brain. The work, though hard and tiring, was very interesting, and I was well satisfied with what I had accomplished. I was also deeply gratified by the expressions of pleasure of the various station masters, who appeared delighted at the prospect of having regular steamer trips to their distant posts and being placed in direct communication with Adelaide, the market for their wool and hides.

At Collendina the black boy deserted and returned to his tribe, some of whom he met in that neighborhood—not quite unexpectedly, for desertion is wholly characteristic of the aborigines. No matter how much they appear to have adopted the white man's civilization, let them but meet one of their old acquaintances and all is forgotten.

They cast away their adopted customs and education with their clothes and return to their original filth and nakedness. As there was really little need of the boy, I decided to continue alone with Everest, rather than try my luck with another native, especially as I had heard much of their natural cupidity and treachery.

Little of importance occurred on the way to Yalama Creek, every day being practically a repetition of its predecessor. The larder was daily replenished with the excellent river cod, perch, bass, and brim with which the water abounded. These are similar to, though not identical with, their American namesakes. Delicious eggs of the wild geese, ducks, and other native birds were plentifully supplied by the natives in exchange for small quantities of flour and tobacco. The blacks along here were very docile and peaceable, being semi-civilized and generally attached to the different stations. They were much interested in Everest's violin and listened to his playing with great pleasure, never having seen or heard such an instru-ment before. They would approach him with curiosity and examine it carefully, remarking, "Takem box, waddy rub him back, makim noise all same him possum."

Below Yalama Creek the Murray is very deep, and its narrow channel winds for some ten or twelve miles between two thickly timbered ridges. These ridges separate it on either side from large lakes, sometimes connected by swamps. Into these the Murray cod go to spawn, and great quantities of them are caught annually and shipped to Echuca, whence they are sent on to various markets, principally Bendigo and Melbourne. During the high water at the wet season these lakes rise and, joining with the river, form one large sheet of water known as Lake Moira in the midst of which the river channel is distinctly marked by the tree tops.

At the time of my surveying trip numerous camps of black fellars were situated along these banks, and I was much interested to watch them paddling about in their mungoes or native bark canoes and spearing fish, which they immediately cooked over a small fire of dry grass and leaves which was always burning in the bottom of the craft. The natives were not the only inhabitants, for numerous dugouts showed the presence of whites engaged in fishing and timber cutting. These dugouts, sixteen or eighteen feet long, are made by halving a large tree trunk and boring holes along the inner surface, which is adzed and burnt out until only a thin shell is left. The ends are then pointed, and the result is an excellent, though heavy, boat.

From Lake Moira to Echuca is some sixty miles. Through this stretch the river shows various characteristics, being wide with low banks in some places and in others running narrowly between high cliffs. At Echuca the river is crossed by a number of rope ferries, over which thousands of sheep are annually passed from New South Wales to Victoria. After Echuca, our next stopping place was Swan Hill, where I had first seen the Murray and where my desire to navigate it was bom.

Below Swan Hill, the Murray is very deep and narrow, its swift current rushing through some very sharp turns called, after one of the early settlers, Cogle's Bends. These turns are so acute that very few of them have not at some time or other felt the nose or stem of a steamer. Having navigated them without mishap, we found the river opening out into a wide stream with long reaches of shallow water. No snags being found along here, we had a good opportunity to admire the scenery and amuse ourselves shooting at the numerous possums which seemed literally to line the banks. These, when properly prepared, are excellent eating. Other wild animals also abounded. The annoying native cat, whose pretty little light brown white-spotted body was often discovered among the provisions (for, although they naturally live on birds, which they secrete in their homes in the hollows of decaying logs, they are great thieves and delight in butter and flour); the cliff-burrowing, tailless, hog-like wombat, whose flesh resembles that of the domestic pig; and the delicious meaty bandicoot, or native rat, the flesh of which reminds one of a sucking pig, and which always adorns the festal Christmas board, all abound in this vicinity.

Although the river continues in much the same character for some distance, it widens perceptibly to the mouth of the Wakool, into which flows the mysterious Edward River. This latter stream, which forms a connecting link between the upper Murray near Yalama Creek and the Wakool, which it enters near the mouth, thus making an island of a portion of the Riverina district, is supposed to have been the original bed of the Murray, and at one time a discussion arose as to which was preferable for navigation. Captain Ebenezer Randall therefore circumnavigated the island in the little steamer *Moolgiwankee* and discovered that the Edward, though navigable for small steamers, was very inferior to the Murray, which was in every way a better stream for commercial purposes.

Between the Wakool and the Murrumbidgee mouths and to some miles below the latter, the banks of the Murray are low and, during the wet season, subject to inundation, which renders them most fertile and finely grassed, making an excellent grazing country. The river is straight here, with long reaches. Nevertheless, to chart it required a great deal of trouble, for the channel is very narrow and exceedingly crooked, owing to the numerous low reefs which run out from either bank, with many spits of shifting sand. It was along here that the fruit of all my labors was nearly lost: we struck an unexpected snag with force enough to put a hole in the bottom of the boat, and my impromptu table was knocked off and the chart thrown into the river. A quick rescue and a hot sun saved the drawings, however, and we soon repaired the boat.

Reaching Wentworth without mishap, we were entertained by old friends and new acquaintances; but we made only a short stop before continuing our journey. Below the mouth of the Darling, the Murray is deep and some three hundred yards in width, with long reaches. As there were no snags, my work was simplified to merely marking the bearings and outlining and describing the banks. So we drifted along without much exertion amid immense flocks of wild ducks (which in this country build their nests in forks of trees, presumably to keep their young well above water-level, as the hatching season occurs at the time of high water), until we came to a large and magnificent bend known as the Devil's Elbow. Here we found the homestead of one John Mackenly, one of the early explorers and pioneer sheep raisers. He entertained us hospitably and showed us over his large and finely stocked station, which occupied a vast area of country. He was much troubled at the time by a small tribe of hostile blacks who made continual depredations on his sheep, although keeping well out of the way of his armed boundary riders.

The Devil's Elbow, or Waponinga, as it is called by the natives, is some eighty feet high and very beautiful, being formed of several strata of distinct colors, ranging from gray at the base to brown at the top, with a red central streak.

Leaving here, we passed the noted Malli Cliffs, so named because covered with malli scrub, which is much used for fuel in this region, its dried roots burning very much like coal. These roots also serve as reservoirs of water for the natives; for, no matter how far the trees seem to grow from the river, their hollow roots always contain pure water. The lazy blacks would rather break the roots to get it than go any distance, however short, for another supply.

When we arrived at Blanchetown we were pretty well tired out; so we decided to make a two days' stop at Rossiter's hotel, where we occupied ourselves in the restful game of skittles—probably the most laborious amusement a lazy man can find in a hot country. However, despite our weariness, we managed to take much pleasure in throwing ten-pound skittles under a corrugated iron roof, while a hot north wind blew upon us through the open side! The hotel and the greater part of this thriving town were situated at the top of a steep hill. There was another small settlement at the foot of the hill, nearer the river, where the hot little iron custom-house was located, presided over by Caleb Peacock, also a representative of the steamboat company.

Leaving Blanchetown, we soon reached a long and magnificent stretch of river known as Moorundi Beach, the right shore being low and wooded, the opposite bank rising precipitously for some one hundred and fifty feet. The cliff is of limestone formation, and the whole face is covered with fossil shells—mostly spirals of the genus *turbo*—which have been crystallized and reflect the sun with dazzling effect. The cliff is surmounted by a well-grassed plateau which extends for miles along the river. At its feet in one place lay a pretty island covered with tall, straight gum saplings, most of which have since been cut off by the government to serve as telegraph poles.

Under the cliff extends an immensely long and narrow cave which, so far as I know, has never yet been fully explored. Although it contains many skeletons, it is supposed to have been an ancient waterway. Everest and I went into this cave for some way, accompanied by Mr. Hayward, owner of the Moorundi station. (The manager of this station, by the way, was a brother of the celebrated Edward Hammond Hargreaves who dis-covered the gold fields at Summer Hill Creek near Bathurst in 1851, for which he was made Commissioner of Crown Lands and given a present of £20,000 by the government of New South Wales. In all, he received above eighty-five thousand pounds, but it did him little good, for he afterward lost it all and was reduced to penury.)

Continuing our voyage, we passed Thompson's Rock, which lies in the center of the river, and upon which stands the only lighthouse on the Murray, near the little town of Wellington, where we stopped for the night. This town is situated upon a treeless plain covered with fine sand, which, during high winds, becomes most disagreeable, blowing through the windows into the houses and even banking against the walls much as snow drifts in colder climes, although not disappearing so obligingly in the hot sun. It is of so shifting a nature that after a hard storm the mail coaches have much difficulty in getting up from Milang.

When we left this hot and disagreeable town our little sail, which had previously served as an awning, was hoisted in its proper capacity, and before a good wind our charting expedition sailed across Lake Alexandrina (so named by its discoverer, the loyal Captain Sturt, in honor of Queen Victoria, then the Princess Alexandrina Victoria of Kent), rounded Point Pomont, and soon saw Mt. Barker rising in the distance, with the little town of Milang lying in the mist.

Here the boat trip ended; for it was decided that, the river from here on being both wide and deep, I could finish the chart to Goolwa from the steamer's deck at some later time. Having been informed by the company's agent that the *Lady Daly* was at Goolwa waiting until favorable news arrived of a rise of the river, we took coach for that place. We passed through Meningie (on Lake Albert, a portion of Lake Alexandrina), which is well known as the location of a famous black mission at which the natives are educated and instructed after the manner of the white man—

which they generally forget, to return to the customs of their ancestors. Arrived at Goolwa, I paid off and dismissed Everest, who soon found employment as cellar-man at Cox's Hotel and played for dances in the evening. I took up my quarters on the *Lady Daly* and awaited instructions from Melbourne, to which place I was soon ordered.

My chart having been inspected and approved by the company, I was installed in my old home at the Globe with orders to make a continuous copy in colors on tracing cloth. When completed some two months later, this first chart of the Murray River was nearly an eighth of a mile long. It was wound on rollers and placed in a glass-faced box in the wheelhouse of the *Lady Daly*, to be reeled off as the steamer proceeded.

7

IT was well into June of 1864 when the river had risen sufficiently for the steamer to start for Albury. Having satisfied my employers with my knowledge of the river, I was ordered to meet her at Echuca as pilot; but, owing to my inexperience in steam-boating, I was placed under Captain Mace and listed as Quartermaster. The trip was a most profitable one; I demonstrated my ability to steer the steamer through all difficulties sufficiently well to show my knowledge of the stream to the satisfaction of the company, and on our return to Goolwa I was made a regular pilot.

Murray & Jackson then owned three river boats; but as the *Settler* was too large to run the upper river successfully, she was sent to Queensland to run the Brisbane from Ipswich to Brisbane, leaving the *Lady Daly* and the *Lady Darling* to operate alternately on the Murray. My orders were to pilot the *Lady Daly* upstream until I met the *Lady Darling*, on which I was to return. But this plan was frustrated by the jealousy of Captain Mace, who, disgusted by the consideration shown me and by some reprimands which he had received for his ignorance of the river, decided to get rid of me. An opportunity soon offered. When we stopped at Blanchetown we were to unload some twenty-five hundred pounds of malt and several large iron tanks. To evade double duty, the malt had been put into the tanks, and it was now necessary to sack it and send it ashore separately, as consigned. As this would require some time, I went ashore with some of the passengers and proceeded to the hotel, where I got into conversation with the company's agent, Mr. Peacock. In the meantime Mace used the utmost dispatch in getting out the cargo and, hastily blowing two shrill blasts on the whistle, moved off. Hearing them, the passengers and I rushed to the wharf in all haste; but when we reached it the boat was calmly steaming up-stream, and all my baggage and my chart were lying on the dock.

I immediately wrote to Mr. Blake, stating the facts, and was recalled to Adelaide while an investigation was being started. While waiting for this to terminate, I received a letter from the Minister of Public Works, stating that he had heard of my chart, which had been highly recommended by a well-known astronomer, Professor Dodd, who had examined it. He wished me to send a copy, and he promised the command of one of the government snag boats at excellent pay. As the chart belonged to Murray & Jackson and they refused permission to copy it, I had to decline this offer.

Some weeks would elapse before the arrival of the *Lady Darling*, to which I was now ordered as pilot, and I seized the opportunity to take a voyage to Madras on the bark *Europa*, under Captain Lindsay, who was carrying a cargo of horses for the British troops there. On my return I was informed that Captain Mace had been transferred to the *Lady Darling* and that Captain Peleg Winiford Jackson, junior partner of the firm of Murray & Jackson, would act as master of the *Lady Daly*, to which I was ordered as pilot.

We had a very successful trip, carrying up a large unconsigned cargo of general supplies, which we sold at good profit to the squatters along the shore, taking in return bailed wool and kegged wine. At Milang the jetty extends out into Lake Alexandrina for nearly a quarter of a mile in very shallow water, for, although the lake is a beautiful basin of nearly thirty miles across, its average depth is only sixteen feet. From this jetty one of our crew caught a Murray cod weighing one hundred and twelve pounds. It was so large that it nearly pulled the man into the water, but his lusty shouts for help were answered just in time to save him a ducking. When this large fish was suspended from a capstan bar through its gills, the bar being supported on the shoulders of two men, its tail dragged on the ground. On its being opened, another cod was found in the stomach weighing six pounds and in so perfect a condition that it was eaten at dinner. This discovery caused an Irishman in the crew to exclaim in amazement: "Begorra, and I niver knew that fishes calved! Sure, and thought they laid eggs!"

On reaching Goolwa, Captain Jackson, who seemed much pleased with my work as pilot, hinted that a master's berth was not far distant. This caused me to refuse various offers as pilot with other lines, as I was very ambitious to appear in a captain's uniform. The three weeks elapsing before another trip I spent with friends in Adelaide, taking part in two vaudeville entertainments for the benefit o f s ome o f m y t heatrical acquaintances.

When the time arrived to return to Goolwa I drove over with Captain Jackson, who, being a member of the firm of Cobb & Company, had at his disposal a pair of fine horses and a good buggy.

After descending Mt. Barker we stopped for breakfast at a little German inn; and here I met with misfortune.

After the meal we went into a little arbor in the garden to smoke; and, there being only one camp-stool in the place, which Jackson took, I reached up and took down a little box from a shelf. I had hardly seated myself, however, when I discovered that it was a beehive. The whole hive swarmed on me, and, mad with pain, I rushed into a little pond nearby, where several duckings finally rid me of the insects.

I made two more successful trips with Jackson, but on the third the river fell so rapidly that we were forced to put in at Blanchetown, where I remained in charge while the Captain returned to Adelaide.

In those days it was not necessary, as it is now, to pass a government examination before the Steam Navigation Board as a preliminary to being allowed command of a river boat. The owners placed in charge whomever they pleased; and, after the many hints from Jackson, I fully expected to be given the command when the river rose. I therefore set my men ashore to cut wood for fuel for the next trip. I was much disgusted when, a few weeks later, Captain Lindsay, with whom I had gone to Madras, appeared with a commission as master, and I was obliged to turn over the boat to him and resume my position as pilot.

After two short trips under this commander, the boat was put out of commission in September, 1864, and moored on the Hindmarsh Flats, all hands being paid off and discharged. Placed on half pay, I went to Adelaide, where I secured employment at McCormick's photographic studio. I remained only a short time; then I went to another photographer named Duryea, whom I taught the art of making ambrotypes, then a novelty in Australia.

It was here that I had my first acquaintance with spiritism, which was then beginning to make itself known on the continent. Mrs. Duryea was subject to clairvoyant trances, during which she seemed to be asleep. On waking she would describe persons and scenes unknown to her in a normal condition. My first experience with this phase was rather star-tling. While I was talking with the lady one day, she suddenly went into a trance; and on waking she said that she had seen my mother, then living in Medford, whom she described perfectly. Sometime afterward, when Mr. Duryea and a party of friends were taking his yacht *Gertrude* up to Lake Alexandrina to enter her in a regatta, Mrs. Duryea, in a state of great excitement, entered the dark-room where I was working and said that she had been in a trance and seen the boat ashore and her husband clinging to the rigging. Nothing that I could say could lull her anxiety. The following morning she received a telegram, "*Gertrude* fast on east bank of Murray, all hands safe"—and that was eighty miles away!

A few weeks completed my association with the Duryeas, for I received orders from Murray & Jackson to return at once to Goolwa and take full command of the *Lady Daly*.

As soon as I received notice of my appointment my youthful vanity induced me to visit the tailor who made me my first uniform. It consisted of a dark blue suit, the coat bearing a double row of gilt buttons, and a blue cap on which the firm cipher was embroidered in gold thread above the British arms. Thus gorgeously apparelled, much to my own admiration, I left Goolwa on the Queen's Birthday of 1865, with an unconsigned cargo of flour, sugar, rice, chaff, and other supplies, which I was to sell at the various stations along the route. The chaff, or cut hay, which was in much demand as fodder, was of two kinds, wheat and oats, and was packed in bags hooped together by sixes to save the South Australian package duty, which imposed a tax of one shilling on every package, regardless of size. The trip was a most profitable one, for the boat was the first to get up the river that season, and supplies were in great demand. I was allowed to make my own prices; and I sold the flour, which cost £10 a ton, and which I was ordered to sell at not less than £40, for £70 without difficulty.

Freights also were then very high, there being no railroad to the upper river, and boats and bullock teams being the only means of transportation. The regular rate was £9 a ton and ten shillings a bale for wool. Four-teen years later, when I left the river, these rates had dropped to fifteen shillings a ton, thanks to the railroad and rapid transit.

On reaching Wentworth the *Lady Daly* left the Murray and steamed up the Darling to Menindee, the nearest river port to the afterward famous Broken Hill, whose immense silver mine was for so long regarded as worthless, but which afterward proved to be exceedingly rich. As this shallow river had never been charted, it required some time to follow its difficult channel; and, the water being low along the Menindee wharf, it seemed advisable to stop the boat some two miles below the town. As I had a number of kegs of English ale which I wanted to sell, I took my chief engineer and walked up to interview Mr. Quinn, the hotel-keeper.

Menindee was then in a primitive state; it consisted of a few huts collected about the barroom and blacksmith shop, all situated on land owned by John O'Shannassy, later Premier of Victoria. The hotel was of the roughest. Its bar was nothing more than a couple of unplaned planks supported by four rough-hewn legs, and the ceiling was formed of calico, which had ripped from its fastenings in places and sagged at the center. The room was filled with men of the toughest variety, who were waiting about for shearing time to come. Many of them were criminals who had been sent out for penal servitude, and all had a virulent hatred of the police, or "blue-bottles," as they called them. As the liquor supply had given out some weeks before, many had taken to ginger wine and Worcestershire sauce to satisfy the morbid cravings of their abnormal stomachs, and they were consequently in a half-crazed condition, filthy, vile, and practically naked.

Mistaking the steamboat uniforms for those of police, the dirtiest and drunkenest of the mob rushed up and struck me squarely in the face. I drew off and knocked him down, while Robinson, my engineer, kicking over the bar, grabbed one of its legs. A free fight ensued, in which the crowd exerted all its power to show the respect in which it held the representatives of Her Gracious Majesty. The battle was shortly ended, however, by Quinn's forcing his way to me, shouting that the boat was in, and explaining the uniforms. The attack immediately ceased, and abject and profuse apologies were in order, my first assailant wishing to kiss me and make up. I managed to evade the fond osculation, and, having sold my ale, continued my course up the Darling.

Stops were made at Ross Read station, where considerable flour was sold, and at Wilcannia, now on the direct road between Sydney and Broken Hill, which passes by the famous Silverton mines, worked much earlier than the richer deposits at Broken Hill. We made a short stop at Fort Bourke and then retraced our course to Goolwa, taking on a large cargo of last season's wool. I turned in so much money that the firm made me a substantial present in appreciation of my services.

As some days must elapse before the new cargo could arrive from Port Elliot and Victor Harbor, whence it was brought by train, I remained on the steamer and occupied my spare time in town. One evening Robinson and I attended an exhibition of mesmerism given at the concert hall of John Farquhar's hotel by an itinerant preacher known as the Reverend Agatha Carr. After giving a rather long and tiresome introduction in which he set forth the theory of mesmerism in a manner as intelligible to his audience as a Maori catechism, he asked four gentlemen from the audience to come to the platform and allow him to demonstrate on them the power of his art. With two others, Robinson and I answered the call and were seated in a row on the front of the stage, each being given a small zinc disk which he was ordered to place in the palm of his hand, and on which he was to concentrate his mind. After succeeding in various attempts on the other two, the reverend gentleman turned his attention to me, made a few passes over my face, and declared that I was then unable to move, although of course I could be lifted from the chair. While he was thus addressing the audience on the power of mind over matter, the mischievous Robinson took from his lapel a large needle which he always carried to sew engine packing and jabbed it through the cane- bottomed chair into my anatomy. Mesmerism immediately lost its power, and with one terrific yell I bounded from my seat and plunged headlong into the lap of an astonished woman in the front row, thus terminating the performance.

Eight miles below Goolwa on the river was a large camp of blacks, who were then engaged in embalming, or rather smoking, the body of their recently defunct old king, Salamandar, a procedure requiring some days to accomplish. One of my firemen, named Willis, who was very friendly with these natives and knew their tribal language, informed the Reverend Carr of this happening and aroused his curiosity to see the process, although it was well known that the aborigines are very exclusive during such rites and suspicious of the whites. Through Willis's influence the affair was arranged, and Carr and I accompanied this friend of the blacks to the camp, where we were allowed in the embalming tent to witness the rites. The honor of smoking or mummifying is not given to all native dead, but is reserved to the corpses of royalty. A large round straw hut is especially built with a hole in its roof for the egress of smoke. In it is erected a scaffold some seven or eight feet in height, upon which the body, already entirely painted with some red concoction especially prepared by the koradjee, or medicine man, and supposedly known to him alone, is placed in a sitting posture with arms and legs crossed. Under this a large fire of dried leaves is kindled, producing little flame, but a thick smoke. It is constantly fed by the mourners, who attend in relays. They sit about the fire, their heads shaven and their entire bodies covered with human excrement, allowing to fall upon them the fat from the drying monarch, which they rub over themselves with great care, constantly chanting a mournful dirge the while. When tired out, they retire to a *mia-mia* nearby for rest, and another relay of grief-stricken subjects relieves them. After the body has thoroughly dried, so that the skin becomes hard and parchment-like, it is carried around with the tribe for two moons, being set up and mourned anew at every camp. It is finally deposited in some hollow tree.

Carr was intensely interested in these funeral rites; and he was anxious to procure the mummy for exhibition on his lecture tour. He offered fifty pounds for it, but without avail, for the indignant and insulted natives, unlike the Scotch troops at Naseby, loyally refused to sell their king, and no amount of palaver could change their decision. Being unable to effect his purpose by purchase, the unscrupulous minister determined to steal the body. At his instigation, on the following day Willis, in spite of the heavy penalty in force against selling or giving spirits to the natives, managed to get the whole camp very drunk. But when he went to get a little cart which he had in hiding for the purpose of removing the corpse, the natives decamped, and on his return he found the place deserted.

The cargo arriving shortly after this affair, three successful but uneventful round trips were made to Albury. During the return on the third, while stopping at Swan Hill, I discovered a very strange little being. As I was leaving Ray's hotel to return to the boat, I saw a curious dwarf sitting at the gate. His torso was that of an average-sized man, and it was surmounted by a large bald head with a Websterian brow, but his arms and legs were extremely short, the legs being only about ten inches in length and without knees. He greeted me with an expansive grin and, rolling over on his large stomach, got up like a dog. On being questioned he replied in a deep bass voice that he had no relatives or friends, that he was about forty years old, and that he had been cooking at the various stations. I was much interested, and, learning that the little fellow was naturally of a humorous disposition and able to sing comic songs very well, I took him down to Goolwa, where he appeared at a concert hall entertainment arrayed in a long-tailed blue coat which gave him the appearance of a kingfisher. He was well received with great applause, and his droll songs and comic sayings were much enjoyed. But it was his only appearance, for on the following night he fell over the side of the boat and, being unable to swim, was drowned. The crew were all below deck and ignorant of the accident, but I learned later that the members of a large Salvation Army camp on the shore had witnessed his death without any attempt to save him, being content to drop on their knees and pray for his soul. The river was dragged all night in vain. Some ten days later the body was found on the Murray Flats, near the river's mouth.

Before leaving Albury for the last trip of the season I entertained my friend Trooper Smith of the police at dinner on board. As we were sitting on deck in the beautiful moonlight enjoying our cigars, he gloomily told me that he was one of a posse which would start the following day in pursuit of the famous bushranger Morgan, who in his general depredations about the country had just struck Harriott's celebrated cattle and sheep station at Round Hill, shooting young Harriott and killing one of his men. It seems that one morning this desperado, who always travelled alone, never having any associates or confederates,—unless the intimidated station owners who sheltered him, through fear, in the districts where he operated may be so considered,— rode upon his beautiful black mare to the Round Hill station and, single-handed, drove all the inmates and employees before him at the points of his pistols into the coach-house. While he was doing it, one of the men foolishly made some derogatory remarks about the bushranger, which incited him to shoot into the crowd. The bullet wounded young Harriott, the only member of the family then present, in the knee. Immediately regretting the accident, Morgan ordered the victim to be carried into the house, where the wound was dressed as well as circumstances allowed, and commanded one of the rounders to ride for the nearest doctor, cautioning him, however, if he valued his life, not to turn from the road or in any way communicate with the police. The rounder started and, not knowing that Morgan was following him, shortly left the road and started at a gallop for the nearest police camp, some two miles distant. He had not gone far when he was overtaken by the bushranger, who, having fired a mortal shot, laid the wounded man across his own saddle and so towed him back to the station, where he died shortly afterward. This murder instigated the police to strenuous endeavor and caused the organization of the posse to which Smith was assigned for duty. The trooper's gloomy presentiment of his coming death was fulfilled. While he was following the fleeing outlaw, Morgan turned in his saddle and shot him dead.

On the return from this trip, a breakage in one of the engines compelled the boat to be laid up along shore for repairs. The neighboring station owner invited me and my only passenger, "King" Foord, to visit the homestead. This landlord was of a type of early Australian ranch-owner which is now fortunately small and fast disappearing. He was a large surly fellow, much inclined to drink. This habit increased his brutality incredibly and extended his naturally bullying disposition to fearful lengths. He boasted of being the man who had taught Morgan how to shoot and started him on his nefarious career of blood and plunder. During our visit, having imbibed freely, he entertained us by trying to pick a quarrel. Being unsuccessful in this, he turned his ill temper on his wife, whom he forced to unlace and remove his shoes and then put them on again. He threw the water-monkey at the unoffending governess, drew a gun to force us to drink, and finally fell on to the veranda in a drunken stupor.

In the morning, far from showing any shame at this conduct, he forced a black boy to mount a vicious horse which he then whipped into throwing and badly injuring the unfortunate jockey; after which he took us to his sister's ranch, a short distance away, and pointed out along the road a number of aboriginal skulls which were placed in the forks of trees, bragging that he had killed the owners. When Foord and I arrived at Goolwa we were not displeased to read in the papers there that he had accidentally shot and killed himself while riding with his wife. We could not refrain from thinking that some outrageous conduct of his had caused the much abused woman to kill him.

As the season for steam-boating was now ended, I discharged all hands and went to Melbourne on half pay to await the rise of the river. While there I appeared in a benefit given to John Ackhurst, the successful author of *The Siege of Troy,* a comic opera just closing a profitable engagement at the Royal Melbourne Theatre. This performance of mine met with unexpected success. Marcus Clarke, author of *The Term of His Natural Life,* then dramatic critic of the Melbourne *Argus,* gave me so favorable a notice that a few weeks later I was invited to assist in a benefit for Miss Annie Ford, one of the favorites of the Royal Melbourne Stock Company, in which I was billed on the posters in large letters as "Captain Augustus B. Pierce, U.S.N."! But, alas for pride, the critics designated my performance as "a few badly sung comic songs which could have easily been dispensed with." This failure did not, however, prevent Coppin, Gravel, and Stuart, proprietors of the Royal Melbourne Theatre, from offering me a permanent position in their stock company, with the intention of sending me to Ballarat to star in *Our American Cousin.*

While I was studying this part and considering the offer, I received a letter from "Anchor" Smith, a well-known steamboat owner, offering me the command of the *Lady Darling,* which he had just purchased and was rebuilding at Echuca under the name of the *Corowa,* in honor of the little town of that name on the opposite shore from Wahgunyah. He promised full pay all the year round and wished me to go to Echuca at once and superintend the construction work. After a consultation with Mr. Blake, who advised me to accept, I resigned command of the *Lady Daly* and severed my connections with the firm of Murray & Jackson.

8

THE *Corowa* was to be run exclusively on the upper Murray, making regular weekly trips between Albury and Echuca, the completion of the railroad to the latter town having reduced the river freight rates below to an amount unprofitable for small boats. Having passed the examinations of the Steam Navigation Board, now required by law, and taken on a mate named Williams who was strongly recommended by Smith, I started the *Corowa* on her first trip to Albury on the rise of the river.

My well-recommended mate proved to be anything but satisfactory; and on the return trip, while passing through the narrow Beebe Bends, he took the opportunity while I was at breakfast to run the boat on a large snag and stave a fourteen-foot hole in her starboard bow. She swung off and filled rapidly, but we were fortunate enough to run her ashore on a sand spit before she settled. The agent at Wahgunyah, being immediately notified, sent up a gang of men to raise the boat and repair the damage. This was accomplished in a few days, and we arrived at Echuca in good condition a little later. This accident resulted rather beneficially than otherwise, for the cargo of wheat had been insured at the full purchase price of ten shillings a bushel, which was collected, whereas in the meantime the market had dropped so that at the time of the wreck wheat was worth only six shillings; the owners were saved four shillings a bushel by the accident. The mishap, however, necessitated my appearance before the local tribunal of the Steam Navigation Board, by which I was fully exonerated. As it was late in the season when the boat had gone into commission, she was now laid off and slipped at Corowa for a thorough overhauling, and

I was free to follow my own inclinations until the rains brought the river up again.

It was at this time that I made the acquaintance of Mrs Bladen Neill, widow of Colonel Bladen Neill, who had been killed a few years before by a fall from his horse at Melbourne. Her ladyship was then living in a bungalow at her large silkworm-raising establishment at Mulberry Farm, and she was spending much time, money, and energy in forming amateur theatrical enterprises which she took on short tours, the proceeds of which were devoted to the various charities in which she was interested. Having heard that I was something of an actor, she invited me to the farm and easily persuaded me to join her company, which was composed of her friends and acquaintances, among whom were the Reverend Mr. Byng, the rector of Corowa, and Mr. Daniels, the banker of the same town. Our first performance took place there, and the piece chosen was *Bluebeard*, a comic opera in which, owing to the smoothness of my face, I played the Princess Fatima, gorgeously dressed in one of her ladyship's gowns ornamented by a beautiful diamond necklace. Mrs Neill appeared as Sister Anne, and the tall and slim Mr. Daniels made a ferocious Bluebeard. At the end of this piece I appeared before the footlights in a Roman toga to give Antony's address to the Romans, which I had half completed when, by prearrangement, the small orchestra struck up a jig, and the orator danced a breakdown in flying toga—much to the amusement of the audience, which howled with delight, but to the great disgust of Mrs Neill, who was very indignant at this "most undignified performance."

We made a short tour through the Ovens District, the Australian El Dorado, playing at Rutherglen, Wangaratta, Beechworth, and other places, for some twelve days in all. The company, with the exception of Lady Neill, whom I drove in a buggy, travelled in a large private coach; and we camped out between stops and had a very jolly time.

On my return from this trip I found the *Corowa* repaired and afloat. My owners not caring to pay my expenses at the hotel, I was given a cook and told to live aboard. This I did for a few weeks; then Mr. Smith discharged the cook for drunkenness and suggested that I do my own culinary work. This double role of master and cook was not at all pleasing to me, and one day when I received word that Smith and his partner were coming to tea I decided that the occasion was propitious for suggesting a change. Accordingly I prepared a meal well calculated to make a lasting impression upon the memories of my guests. I concocted some wonderful cakes of every ingredient to be found in the galley—flour, eggs, ginger, syrup, raisins, and various spices. When nicely browned they wore a most appetizing appearance—which was wholly deceitful, for it was utterly impossible to make any impression on their adamantine surfaces. After vainly striving to masticate these most durable articles, which were better suited for a theatre property room than a human stomach, the guests resigned the task and asked about the composition of the fossils. I told them that they were called "main truck cakes"; and when I repeated the list of ingredients, Smith decided that it was cheaper to board me than to provide galley supplies. So I went to Wahgunyah and put up at the hotel kept by Camille Reau, a son of sunny France.

One morning I, with some others, was leaving the hotel for a day of duck shooting, when one of the party called my attention to a goat feeding on the opposite side of the road and dared me to take a shot at it. I raised my gun, without intending to pull the trigger. My companion gave me a vigorous slap on the back; the gun discharged with a loud report and a strenuous kick which threw me to the ground; the goat wiggled his tail and bounded from view; and four panes of glass crashed to pieces in a neighboring deserted house. The door of this house immediately opened, and two "sundowners" (tramps) rushed out, crying: "Don't shoot! Don't shoot! We give ourselves up!" A police trooper, hearing the noise, came running up. He accepted our explanation and allowed us to proceed about our busi-ness, but carried off the sundowners to the police camp. The following morning I was summoned before the local court on the charge of violating the peace by discharging firearms in the main thoroughfare. In defense I gave a truthful, though humorous, relation of the occurrence; and the stipendiary magistrate not only dismissed the case, but complimented me so highly upon capturing the two vagrants, who were wanted for petty larceny, that I was rather disappointed at not receiving the Victoria Cross for my work.

At this time Wahgunyah was celebrated for the establishment known as the Endeavour Dance Hall, which was kept by a man named Marshall, generally known as "Old Forty," which had been his number when he was shipped from England as a convict to the Australian penal settlement. In this temple to Terpsichore all who danced must drink, and each round of homage to the muse ended in a libation to Bacchus. This was insisted upon by "Old Forty," who was constantly on the watch, strolling about the room with a peter of loaded dice and a pack of greasy cards with which he lambed down many a foolish young fellow.

During this period of enforced idleness, I occupied much time in travelling about the vicinity and seeing the country. I visited the extensive gold fields at Beechworth. There I met "Lucky" Johnson, who, though an ignorant and illiterate fellow, had made a vast fortune in a short period and was spending it in what he considered a princely manner, going so far as to have his favorite saddle-horse shod with golden shoes. He increased his notoriety and popularity by a farewell banquet which he gave just before leaving the country to return to his native land, at which there were many plates piled with sandwiches the fillers of which were one-pound notes!

Beechworth was later prominent as the locality of many depredations of the famous Kelly gang. While travelling from here to Buckland I passed the spot where, a short time before, the police had discovered the daring bushranger Power fast asleep and forced him to surrender. Although he had never been known to kill anyone, his bold robberies had caused great excitement in the neighborhood, and he was taken to Wangaratta, where he was tried and sentenced to life imprisonment for robbery under arms. Some fifteen years later he was pardoned out on his offer to assist the police in capturing the notorious Kelly brothers, but he failed to accomplish anything, and finally, old and broken in health, he disappeared. His dead body was later found on the Murray bank at Swan Hill.

Buckland was then past the height of its glory, its rich alluvial diggings having been abandoned as devoid of ore; and at this time its innumerable pits were filled with Chinamen. These sons of the celestial empire always enter mining towns as the white men leave; and often, by industry and care, they acquire fortunes from supposedly worked-out fields deserted by their former owners as worthless. Here I saw the first snow since leaving my New England home; it was on the peak of a high mountain near

Snowy River. The mountain was known as the Buffalo. I travelled its precipitous side by coach and on foot.

Learning that the river was rising, I returned to Corowa and again made my weekly trips. Toward the end of the season, the water having fallen considerably, it was necessary at one place to put a large portion of the cargo ashore so as to lighten the boat sufficiently to heave it across an obstructing reef, after which the goods were carried along the bank and reshipped. But even this was of slight avail, for we were only able to make Boorhaman, where we were obliged to stop. My familiarity with the river led me to believe that some days would elapse before further way could be made; so I decided to go overland to Rutherglen to see a certain young lady in whom I was interested. I left the boat in charge of Mate Williams and, procuring a horse from John Hay, M.P., owner of one of the finest stations in the Riverina district, rode over for a short visit. But, by a fitful variation from its usual habit, the river started to rise suddenly and with such rapidity that by the time I had finished my fond farewells and reached the *Corowa* it had gone up some five feet. I learned to my dismay that Captain Bower's *Little Riverina,* belonging to a rival company, had passed and was ahead. Fortunately for me, Bowers got out of the channel at Terramia Paddock, and I managed to get my boat into Wahgunyah first, but much later than was expected. On returning to Echuca, I was severely reprimanded and dismissed by Anchor Smith, who had learned the cause of my tardiness; and the *Corowa* went out on her next trip in command of a Mr. Thompson, while I went overland to Wahgunyah to await the offer of another berth.

Some days later, hearing the approach of the boat, I went down to the wharf, where the *Corowa* arrived three days late, minus her wheelhouse and smokestack, and in fact a perfect wreck above the water. Her commander had lost the channel at Lake Moira and got too near the shore, where the trees had inflicted a heavy penalty on his incompetency. Smith immediately offered to reemploy me on condition that I get married; so I hastened to bring my fiancee down from Rutherglen. We were wedded at Moama, across the river from Echuca, in the summer of 1867, and I was reinstated in command of the now repaired *Corowa*.

Money being a desirable article for a newly wedded pair, I sought to increase my funds during the dry season by sending my wife to visit her mother at Sydney, while I shipped as quartermaster under Captain William McLean on the old *Korong*, making a round trip from Melbourne to Adelaide. After this I shipped on the barque *Pepper* for a trip to Batavia, Java, and Singapore, returning through the Straits of Malacca with a stop at Sumatra.

I reached Adelaide just in time to see the Adelaide cup run at Hindmarsh (named for the first governor of Adelaide), where I met many of my old Melbourne friends and attended the luncheon of the club stewards. I also went to the banquet at the Globe Hotel as the guest of Mr. James Wilson, well known as the breeder of some of the finest horses in Australia. At this banquet, Harry Figg, better known in racing circles as "the Glutton"—he had once accomplished on a wager the feat of eating twenty-one veal pies—consumed among other things a whole sucking pig weighing between six and eight pounds.

As it was now time to put the *Corowa* into commission, I went to Melbourne to interview Mr. Smith. To oblige Mr. Wilson I carried over his fine trotter Westberry, a handsome light chestnut of about sixteen hands, which I left at Emerald Hill, my first landing place on the Australian continent. During the interview with Mr. Smith, I referred to the back pay due me according to the agreement of full pay all the year round. He informed me that that stipulation referred only to my first engagement and not to the second, and that therefore there was nothing due me. This remark led to an argument, and I received my final discharge from the service of the Smith interests.

Thinking this a good opportunity to visit my wife, who was staying at Glebe Island on the Parramatta River, I immediately took passage for Sydney on the *Koonwara*. Landing at Circular Quay, I took a cab and enjoyed a long and pleasant drive. I passed, among other things, the Pymont quarries, noted for the production of beautiful freestone, of which most of the public buildings of Sydney are constructed. When, four hours later, I finally crossed the fine bridge over the Parramatta, I learned to my disgust that I might have crossed by the ferry near the quay and walked the whole distance in twenty minutes.

My short stay here was occupied in visiting places of interest, among which were the beautiful Parramatta orange groves, the large abattoirs at Glebe Island (which, being over the water, are constantly surrounded by hundreds of sharks), the prison at Cockatoo Island, and the lunatic asylum at Bedlam.

Having no doubts of my ability to get command of another river boat, I left Sydney, accompanied by my wife, shortly before the expected rise of the Murray. We went by train, passing through the long stretch of beautiful orange groves, crossing the Blue Mountains, and descending the steep face of Mount Victoria over the celebrated zigzags which terminate in the lovely Lithgow valley. We detrained at Rydal and made the trip to Echuca by stage coach in some six days. Shortly after my arrival I was given command of a fine large side-wheeler, the *Jane Eliza* (Smith & Banks), which was to make weekly runs between there and Albury. Mrs. Pierce accompanied me for several trips, until I found a house for her at Echuca.

This town is situated upon the point of the peninsula at the junction of the Campaspe with the Murray, and during exceptionally high water it is liable to inundation. During the high water of 1868, when the river rose extraordinarily, a bad flood occurred, and upon returning from one of my trips I was obliged to take one of my boat and rescue my wife and small son from the second story of our house and remove them to the Town Hall, which, being on higher ground, was only about two feet under water.

On the fall of the river after my second season with the *Jane Eliza,* my friend Kendall, who was much impressed by the great financial success of Batchelder's splendid panorama of the American Civil War, which was then touring the country, instigated me to paint a panorama called *A Voyage Around the World,* to be shown about the district during the low season. The work consisted of twenty-four six-by-nine-foot can-vases. The series began with a copy of Frith's great painting of Paddington Station, London. It went on to show the arrest by Scotland Yard officials of Redpath, the famous railway defrauder who was afterward banished to Western Australia; presented scenes of Madeira, the Ascension Islands, St. Helena, and Cape Town; and ended with a view of Melbourne. When completed the canvas was about two hundred and twelve feet long. It was placed on rollers. Two stage scenes were painted; and, provided with a remodelled old fish wagon and a pair of horses, Pierce & Kendall's pan-orama was prepared to start on its tour of the colonies. We met with excel-lent results, showing at Moama, Redbank, Boraga, Koonoomoo, Corowa, Wahgunyah, Howlong, Albury, Wodonga, and Beechworth. At the last-named we gave a benefit for the local hospital, and were rewarded with a life membership in the institution.

Our next stop was at Wangaratta, where I first saw the famous Kelly gang. Four young fellows arrayed in strapped riding breeches and boots, with white boiled shirts, narrow ties, and cabbage-tree hats of the regular larrikin type, occupied the front row and were very annoying with their loud comments and general behavior. Kendall, who was lecturing, requested them either to be quiet or leave, both of which suggestions they refused. A police trooper then quietly warned Kendall to be careful, as one of them was Dan Kelly himself, and they all had bad records for cat-tle-duffing and other depredations. During the intermission Kendall and I met them at the hotel bar and managed to ingratiate ourselves sufficiently to win their approval and cause them to appear the following night with a large crowd of friends, which substantially increased our receipts. At this place we changed our old wagon for a comfortable jack coach in which we could travel with more ease and dignity.

In this we proceeded to Peechebla, where we were entertained at the station of Mr. George Rutherford. He told me of the death there, a few weeks previously, of the famous bushranger Morgan, which was the sole topic of conversation in the neighborhood.

Morgan had confined his depredations largely to New South Wales, and it was often said that he did not dare to visit Victoria, whose vigilant police would soon capture him. The outlaw took up the challenge and by some means made a wager that he would cross the border alone, visit the important towns and stations, and return to New South Wales in safety.

One evening while the Rutherford household, consisting of Mr. Ruth-erford, his wife, Mr. Ewen McPherson and his son, and Mrs. Dufrere, a daughter of McPherson who was married to Rutherford's manager, were at dinner, a knock was heard at the door. When it was answered by the servant, Morgan appeared, armed to the teeth, and drove the whole household into the parlor, where he kept them at the point of a pistol. He informed them that he intended no harm, but sought only entertainment. If they would treat him well, he would ride away in the morning without causing any disturbance; but he warned them that, if any movement were made to notify the police of his presence, he would murder them all. Then, comfortably ensconcing himself at one end of the parlor, he ordered food and drink, which he forced the others to taste before he would touch it; and with a full stomach he settled down to enjoy a pleasant evening. He obliged the family to amuse him with conversation, and Mrs. Dufrere played the piano for hours. In fact, after the first fright had passed away the whole family did their best to propitiate their unwelcome guest.

Meanwhile the servant girl, who was allowed to pass freely in and out while serving the bushranger, managed to send a small boy to the police camp at Wangaratta with information of Morgan's presence; so that when morning arrived the place was surrounded by hidden troopers, who, not daring to make themselves known, were awaiting their victim in ambush. At daybreak, thanking his host for the entertainment, Morgan requested Mr. McPherson and his son to accompany him to the saddling paddock, as he desired to exchange his black mare for a fresh horse. While they were on their way thither, Quinlan, the only employee who was not away on the cattle round-up, managed to secrete himself with a rifle behind a large gum tree on the path; and just as Morgan passed he shot him in the back, inflicting a mortal wound. The bushranger immediately dropped unconscious; but while he was being disarmed this desperate villain came to and murmured, "Coward, to shoot a man in the back!" although he had never hesitated to do the same thing himself. These dying words made so great an impression on Quinlan that, shortly after receiving the large reward paid for Morgan's capture dead or alive, the unfortunate fellow became insane.

The outlaw was hardly dead when the police, brave enough now that there was nothing more to fear, bounded into the path, followed by a large number of people. Among them was an excited photographer who, in his eagerness to secure a portrait of the body, broke his camera while climbing the fence. However, with the aid of some brown paper the damage was soon repaired, and the corpse, propped up against some bales in the wool house, was photographed between the McPhersons. The Superintendent of Police at Beechworth ordered that Morgan's face be skinned, so that he might preserve the magnificent black beard as a trophy. This was done, but it cost the official his position, for his superiors, disgusted at his barbarity, immediately reduced him to the ranks. The body was decapitated. Those who had charge of the large cemetery situated on the road from Wangaratta to Peechebla refusing burial within the enclosure, a grave was dug just outside the fence; and there on the public highway repose the remains of him whose very name had been a terror to the surrounding country. The head was sent to Melbourne that a cast might be made of it, but through some oversight of the express agent it was mislaid and was not discovered until it was too late to preserve any outline of the features.

Being convinced that the panorama was a source of greater profit than steam-boating, I resigned my position with Smith & Banks and, refusing numerous offers from other firms, left the river for a while and turned my attention to new fields.

9

A VOYAGE Around the World started its second tour from Albury with a successful launching and a very complimentary notice in the Albury *Banner*, and thence moved on to The Posts, a little village consisting only of a hotel and post office, but considered a good show place because surrounded by a number of sheep runs from which the men were always inclined to come to any sort of entertainment. We next showed at Wagga Wagga, Tarcutta on the Murrumbidgee, and at the large mining camp at Adelong. When we rode down the long hill into Gundagai, late one afternoon, we were delighted to see a great number of people walking toward the town, dressed in their best clothes. We expected a large and profitable audience; but, alas, we were soon disillusioned, for we learned that they were looking for different recreation. They were bound for a mission held that evening by the Reverend Father McCarthy of Deniliquin. We now followed the Murrumbidgee to a point opposite Jugiong, where the river is very wide and shallow, with a muddy and difficult ford. This we crossed with the additional aid of a bullock team. Then, crossing the mountains, we reached Carcoar, where we showed to a good house in spite of having to run in opposition to Burton's Circus. Our next stop was at Cowra, where we performed in the Court House to the harmonious strains of an old Hamlin organ lent by the schoolmaster. There being no stage here or any suitable stand for the lecturer, the police trooper in charge of the building thoughtfully dragged forward a large box for my accommodation. The night was very hot, and gradually the hall became permeated with a most disagreeable odor, which, becoming unbearable, made me abbreviate my lecture considerably and bring the show to an early close.

After the audience had departed I questioned the trooper as to the cause of the unpleasantness, and was informed that the box on which I had been standing contained the mortifying remains of a man found dead some days before. They were being kept for the inquest to be held the following morning!

From Cowra we passed through a number of mining towns and camps, meeting many small parties of blacks who begged "baccy" and sugar, to Bathurst on the Macquarie River (so named for Governor Lachlan Macquarie, "the Prisoners' Friend," who affixed his own name or a name out of his own family to nearly every place in New South Wales discovered between 1810 and 1821, his term as governor). Bathurst had been founded as a penal settlement, but a flourishing city had now grown up around its once isolated penitentiary.

Kendall's health being poor, we dissolved partnership. But as I retained the pictures, I showed alone to some very good houses. Presently I met Mr. David Brown, whose son-in-law, Mr. Hugh Hamilton, being interested in the panorama business, had started a series of paintings of the Franco-Prussian War. As Hamilton was not particularly successful as an artist, Mr. Brown, who was financing the venture, engaged me to paint the panorama. When completed three months later, it consisted of twenty-five ten-by-twelve-foot canvases. Having finished this work, I again started out with my own show, to which I added two singers billed as Woodie & Moffitt, the latter being the wife of a celebrated Beechworth jockey. I intended to make a tour of the rich mining district of Tambaroora; but, meeting with slight success, I dismissed my support and returned to Bathurst, where I painted a number of pictures illustrating Artemus Ward's humorous writings and prepared a lecture on the same. So equipped, I again attempted to tour the gold fields. I opened at Orange. But the Australian sense of humor was too near akin to its British mother to be capable of caring for Artemus Ward; and the venture fell flat. I returned to Bathurst, leaving the paintings for my hotel bill; and on sending for them I received them in an utterly ruined condition—they had been transported uncovered during a heavy rain.

I was still enamored of the show business and bound to continue in it. I at once set to work and produced a number of small miscellaneous pictures. Then I formed a partnership with a man named Chapman and, having reengaged Woodie and Moffitt, started again for the gold fields. We showed to good houses at Mudgee, Gulgong, Home Rule, and Tambaroora, and returned by Box Ridge, The Reefs, and Orange to Bathurst, making a successful month's tour. Our second trip was made through Victoria and Hill End, but as the alluvial gold had been seemingly all collected and the district was considered thoroughly worked out, many of the reefs had been abandoned and the field largely deserted, rendering the ground unfit to bear a financial crop for panorama entertainments, and we returned to Bathurst very short of funds. A few weeks later we learned that our trip had been a little premature: fortune, always uncertain and especially so in connection with mining property, took a sudden turn and a great gold boom broke out at Hill End. Two Germans, Beyers and Holtermann, had for more than eight years been patiently working a seemingly worthless claim on Hawkins's Hill, living in a cave there and spending odd moments in repairing clocks, watches, and jewelry in order to keep body and soul together, while they industriously dug away with Teutonic perseverance at their unyielding mine. Suddenly their tireless efforts were rewarded by the opening of a large and exceedingly rich vein. The news of their fortune, which lost nothing by the length of its journey, soon reached Sydney, together with rumors of rich findings on other claims; and Hill End experienced a startling boom. Thousands of the shifting, adventur-ous, fortune-seeking part of the population flocked to the district to take out five- and ten-acre leases under the mining acts, followed by the usual collection of sundowners, gamblers, rum-sellers, and storekeepers which is ever present during such times. Claims which could not have been given away forty-eight hours before were now easily floated for fabulous sums.

At this time I met an old friend from Ballarat, William B. Gill, journalist, dramatist, and actor, who some twenty years later moved to Chicago and there gained an enviable reputation. Gill had decided to go to Hill End and open a theatre, and as I had then separated from Chapman he invited me to enter a partnership with him to that end. A few days later we were on our way to the diggings in search of quarters wherein to open business. The weather was hot and the journey tiresome, for we were obliged to climb the steep face of Monkey Hill over a straight dirt road, very unlike the splendid zigzag which now renders the passage comparatively easy. As no building of sufficient seating capacity was to be found, we were much pleased to learn that a large tent with corrugated iron sides and canvas top was for sale at Tambaroora, some four miles away. On further inquiry it was found to be forty by eighty feet square, with a nine-foot wall, and in excellent condition. We effected its purchase for sixty pounds through the assistance of the well-known Jerry Dwyer, or, as he was more commonly called, "Jerry the Jingler." This man had been, a year previously, a poor and struggling miner; but he had been so fortunate as to strike gold, and now he was the sole owner of one of the richest claims at Hill End. In addition to his mining interests he was a large manufacturer of soda waters and temperance cordials, and he agreed to advance us a hundred pounds if we would open a spa in our theatre and sell only his products. This we did. Little difficulty occurred in procuring a site on which to erect the tent, for Clyne, the hotel-keeper, was very glad to give land enough adjoining his hostelry on the main and only street, so that he might benefit from the thirst of the theatre patrons.

After much trouble in transporting the tent, which, owing to the poor conditions of the roads—they were utterly unfit for wagon traffic—had to be packed on the backs of horses, it was finally erected and filled with seats made by driving posts into the ground and placing boards across them. The orchestra consisted of an old three-legged square Collard & Collard piano the missing leg of which was replaced by a porter case. The two extant panoramas were shipped up from Bathurst to act as scenery, and the Theatre Royal opened a week later to a packed house which represented not more than half of those who wanted to get in.

The entertainments consisted principally of local farces written by Mr. Gill. They introduced local characters and scenes from mining life. The author's wife, an excellent actress who appeared under the name of Deering, played the leading female roles; the playwright himself assumed the important male parts, supported by an ever changing company of average worth. I was the principal vaudeville artist, and I gained some popularity by my legerdemain, monologues, comic songs, and ventriloquism.

Although many of the profession who drifted to the Theatre Royal from various parts of the earth were not lacking in talent and ability, there were also some whose work could not bear out their pretensions.

Among these latter was one John Longford, a discharged warden of the Darlinghurst jail at Sydney, who asserted that his handsome face and fine voice had won him success in vaudeville under the name of "Joe Baxter of the Pacific Slope," although he admitted that he had never set foot on American soil. The theatre, being then short of talent, engaged him, and he appeared between the acts for a short song and dance. After performing *Josephus Orange Blossom* in a fairly acceptable manner, he essayed a clog dance. During it his immense feet became unmanageable, and he fell over the footlights on to the orchestra, knocking over and breaking six kerosene lamps in his course and setting fire to the stage. I was acting as stage manager. I rushed on with two buckets of water, which I poured over the burning oil. It ran quietly through the piano and over the legs of the pianist, who immediately jumped up and fell over the prostrate form of the unfortunate dancer. The sight of the fire terrified the audience of the crowded and inflammable theatre and almost created a panic. But the efforts of the management succeeded in reassuring them and enabling everybody to move out in an orderly manner, to the strains of *God Save the Queen*, which I pounded out of the water-soaked piano in a manner rarely heard. Baxter was dismissed, much to his chagrin. But he soon found employment aiding the old sexton of the Hill End church in digging graves; and he proved much more useful to the dead than he had been in amusing the living.

When the Theatre Royal had been in operation about six weeks, the large and well-appointed Constable Guggenheim theatre was ready for business; and as we had a good opportunity to sell out our business, we did so and dissolved partnership.

I then took out a miner's writ and secured a quarter-acre claim, on which I erected a small tent and settled down to await the results of a mining venture in which I was interested. A company had been formed by myself, Gill, and two others, which had taken up a ten-acre lease of a slightly worked claim on Box Ridge, and one of our number was sent to Sydney to interview Little and Pyle, mining agents, in an endeavor to float the claim. But before this could be done the great boom was beginning to decline, and purchasers were growing wary. The company's representative at Sydney hastened back to the diggings with the unpleasant information that the chances for sale were daily diminishing, but that he had found a customer for £400. He strongly advised the acceptance of the offer, especially as the lease had cost us almost nothing and none of us could afford to work it. Gill and I readily agreed and sold our holdings for eighty pounds each. We were much chagrined a few days later to discover that the mine had been actually sold to Major Shepard of Sydney for £2200— the balance having presumably been shared by the others.

However, as I had been earning some twelve or fifteen pounds daily in surveying and draughting the various mining claims about me, I decided to remain. I built a three-room wattle-and-daub house and sent for my family. This house was constructed in regulation style, without sills, by simply driving saplings into the ground at regular intervals, on either side of which were fastened the wattles or split limbs, forming horizontal half-rounds, the space between them being filled in solid with a mixture of earth, water, and grass. The roof was made of saplings and gum bark, and a chimney erected of slabs and finished with a barrel. A trench was then dug around the hut to drain off the water, and the new residence was complete. For interior decoration I used such portions of the *Artemus Ward* panorama as had not been water-soaked; Brigham Young and his numerous progeny gazed down from the bedroom ceiling, keeping watch like guardian angels; and different views of Salt Lake around the walls enlarged the perspectives of the different rooms. When everything was ready Mrs. Pierce and the children came up from Sydney, and we settled down to domestic life in a dwelling which thousands of cockatoos never allowed to become lonesome.

After the bursting of the boom,—it was largely due to the uncompromising honesty of Holtermann, who paid the penalty of his virtues, even to finding his life threatened and being burned in effigy,—the greater part of the undesirable element went away, and the owners of the legitimate mines began regular work. The numerous unfortunates who had exchanged good money for worthless claims gradually dwindled away, leaving thousands of pounds' worth of valuable machinery to lie rusting and idle.

About this time Sir Hercules G. R. Robinson, Governor of New South Wales, in making a tour through his territory, visited Hill End. A committee of citizens of which I was a member was appointed to arrange a programme for his reception and entertainment. Two of the committee were sent down the road to meet him, the rest awaiting his arrival at Coyle's hotel. As the gubernatorial carriage drove up to the door, the waiting crowd burst into song, it having been prearranged to greet him with the strains of *God Save the Queen*. But Shepard, the local editor, who was leading the chorus, in his excitement pitched the key in a high falsetto which no one could reach, and the stanza died away in awful discord. His Excellency stood up in his carriage, hat in hand, bowing his immense and rotund body at regular intervals while he wiped his bald and shining head, on which the merciless noontide sun was fiercely beating. He tried to look calm and dignified; but an expression of relief was seen to pass over his features when no attempt was made to begin the second stanza of the national anthem.

Regardless of temperature and time, Sir Hercules was escorted about the diggings and finally led back to the hotel, where a banquet was given in his honor at which all the local dignitaries took an opportunity to display their oratorical powers. The speech-making was closed by the magistrate, who was so overwhelmed by the dignity of the governor that he said "Your Excellency" at every other word. He began: "Your Excellency, while we had hoped, Your Excellency, that you might have visited us earlier, Your Excellency, we are, Your Excellency, delighted to receive you now, Your Excellency. A year ago, Your Excellency, at the time, Your Excel—" But he was interrupted by one of the committee, who, having imbibed too freely in an endeavor to moisten the many preceding dry speeches, reared a long lank form above the table and appealed to the Governor with, "Your Excellency, will you kindly instruct that damned fool to close his features, Your Excellency?" This broke up the dinner, and Sir Hercules continued his journey, with many expressions of satisfaction at his entertainment.

Having enjoyed some eight months of successful draughting, I was now obliged to seek another occupation; for mine-owners began to refuse to employ me on the plea that I was not a licensed surveyor and that therefore claims based on my work would not be recognized in case of legal difficulties. However, the quality of my work was appreciated by the licensed surveyors, and some of the best firms offered me employment. But, having accumulated a neat little sum of money, I declined their offers and for the succeeding three or four months divided my time between painting another panorama and gathering small quantities of alluvial gold from my little claim.

While I was so employed one very sultry afternoon, the town was visited by an earthquake. Although it lasted some ten seconds and caused much excitement among the populace, it produced no gap. It could not have had any very deep effect, for none of those working underground in the deep claims had noticed it.

Gus Pierce's theatre tent on Clarke Street, Hill End, 1872.

Gus Pierce and his son (fourth left) outside Tattersall's Hotel, Hill End, 1872.

10

ABOUT this time Holtermann's mine produced a nugget of slate, quartz, and gold four feet high and from nine to twelve inches thick, which was purchased by the Victoria Bank at Sydney for £5000. Before shipping it, Holtermann exhibited it for the benefit of the Hill End Hospital. Desiring to procure, for use in my panorama, one of the photographs which had been taken of Mr. Holtermann and his immense nugget, I called on that wealthy miner. He became much interested in my work and not only allowed me to paint a life-size portrait of himself, in his shirt-sleeves, beside the find, but permitted me to erect a canvas studio at his mine, in which to paint as many scenes of mining life as I desired. When this work was finished it consisted of twenty-two six-by-nine-foot canvases illustrating mining life, pastoral scenes, and the habits and customs of the aborigines. It was entitled *The Mirror of Australia*. Mr. Holtermann was so greatly interested in the production, which he wished me to show about the country, that he presented me with a pair of horses and a very good coach, large enough to accommodate the whole family. I accordingly sold my wattle-and-daub hut to the village blacksmith and prepared to start on another tour. As I did not consider the panorama sufficient to supply an evening's entertainment,

I had illustrated Bret Harte's celebrated poem, *The Heathen Chinee*, which was to be rolled off as I repeated the stanzas.

We opened at Hill End to an excellent house, despite the fact that Batchelder arrived at the same time with his religious *Feast of Heaven* and his much lauded panorama of the Civil War. We then moved on to Peel, Bathurst, Gulgong, and Home Rule. The trip was not successful, owing to the fact that we had unfortunately chosen a tour that duplicated Kelley and Hussey's Minstrels, and the towns could not support both. I therefore abandoned the business at Home Rule and formed a contract with Joe Morse, proprietor of the Ring of Bells, by which I was to use my team and coach in making daily trips between Gulgong and Home Rule—a distance of seven miles through a marshy country—to carry passengers and mail. Three months of this work convinced me that it was profitless, there being but little mail matter and small passenger traffic. I was undecided about continuing the arrangement, when a new rush broke out some fifty miles away, at Jaw Bone on the Macquarie River, on the road to Dubbo.

Morse suggested that it might be advisable to go there and investigate the prospects for establishing a hotel or theatre (having been a clown in Burton's Circus, he felt qualified for either). I readily agreed; and two days later we were driving the whole outfit through the woods, past many black camps, to Jaw Bone—meeting, as always happens at such times, many of the weak-hearted and easily discouraged, who were returning with tales that it was all a fake and that no gold had been found.

On arriving at the diggings we learned that the Gold Warden had not yet arrived and that therefore no claims could be taken up. According to the Australian mining laws, when prospectors found gold on any government land they were obliged to take it to the Gold Warden of that district to be assayed. If he found it worthy of further consideration, he visited the ground to investigate its yielding capacity. If this proved satisfactory, the date of opening was set and well-advertised, and the claims laid out in blocks sixteen feet square. On the appointed day those desiring to possess claims stood ready, pegs in hand, and when the Warden gave the signal they rushed to peg out their property. As more than one person was often desirous of the same claim, many immediate fights ensued, and many long and bloody feuds were thus established.

As the Warden was not expected until the next day, we walked about the town to see what was going on and to decide what it was best to do. Many little calico houses and canvas shops had been erected for the sale of provisions and liquors, and numerous bark houses were springing up all along the road. Although there was plenty of canned stuff to be bought, there was no fresh bread; which fact decided us to build a bakery. I immediately started to erect a bark-and-sapling hut. Morse went back to Home Rule, whence he returned in two days bringing with him Scottie, his excellent baker from the Ring of Bells, a quantity of boards, and the necessary supplies for a bakery. In the meantime I had nearly finished a twenty-by-thirty hut, and but little was required to complete it. The oven was constructed with walls of field stone over-arched with sheets of corrugated iron covered with clay. The slabs for the floor were obtained without difficulty by Scottie, who appropriated for that purpose the desired number of tombstones from the old prison burial ground, a few miles distant at Wellington, which had formerly been a large penal settlement. The Jaw Bone Bakery opened to a rushing business and prom-ised to be a great success. The demand for bread was steady; and as the little settlement grew from four hundred to ten thousand in less than a fortnight, the business increased rapidly. The town took on an entirely different appearance. Bark houses appeared along new streets, dance halls and dram shops became numerous, and the varied sounds of squealing fiddles, yelling drunkards, squalling children, and barking dogs mingled with the incessant pounding of hammers and sawing of boards.

On the opening day Morse and I had pegged out a claim apiece and purchased four more from different peggers along the same lead, all a short distance from our bakery. We put some fellows to work on it to prevent having it jumped; for, according to the mining laws, unless a claim be constantly worked its title is void, and it may be taken by anyone willing to mine it. As is usual in alluvial deposits, this lead followed the dry bed of an old stream. It was only some sixty feet deep, with considerable surface gold under the sod. We installed a common windlass with bullock-skin bucket, and began the sinking of a shaft.

But, with all the excitement and industry, very little gold was being found. The prospectors had decamped and their claims been jumped. Suddenly the cry of "Fake!" went up, and rumors began to be circulated that the prospectors' claim had been salted—that the Warden had been imposed upon, and that there was no gold. Faith gave way to suspicion, and suspicion turned to fear, and the boom was ended. The population dwindled away almost as rapidly as it had advanced; and, after three months of the most flourishing success, the bakery business was no longer profitable. Provisions became scarce and supplies stopped. We sold out our claim for a few pounds and dissolved partnership. Morse returned to the management of his Ring of Bells, and I again stowed the *Mirror of Australia* in my coach and started with my family to Wellington.

We showed to excellent houses there for a week. During this time I became acquainted with the warden of the jail, who, having held his position for over fifty years, was able to give a vast amount of information about the treatment of convicts in the old days of the penal colony, when hundreds were sent out for minor offenses such as petty larceny and poaching, and for political reasons. As a graphic illustration of the old convict life as recounted by the warden, the following is typical: A gang of convicts was felling trees a short distance from the jail. One of them was crushed to death by a falling trunk. His body had hardly touched the ground when one of his comrades inserted his fingers between the lips of the dying man and deftly extracted the partially chewed cud of tobacco, which he immediately appropriated to his own comfort and pleasure.

Leaving Wellington, we continued up alongside the Macquarie to Dubbo, then a great cattle center. There we showed for a few days, during which we camped on the river bank about three miles above the town. One afternoon while driving a coach load of supplies up from Dubbo, I was overtaken by a most terrific electric storm, accompanied by an exceedingly high wind. Despite all efforts to reach camp before it broke, I arrived too late and found the tents blown to ribbons, my property scattered before the gale, and my family standing unprotected in the road amidst a hailstorm, the individual stones of which were as large as hens' eggs. Inside of five minutes the storm had passed, and the hot sun was drying us off. Enough punk was secured from the insides of hollow trees to start a fire, and supper was soon prepared. A party of blacks coming along most opportunely, we purchased from them a large fish of some seven pounds, of a species which resembles the American hornpout and tastes like an eel. The natives call them "debbil-debbil" and refuse to eat them, saying that "they are all same lika boree," or evil spirit.

Soon after this event we left Dubbo and retraced our steps through Gulgong, Mudgee, and Orange to Lambing Flats (so named from its landlords' custom of securing all the loose change of their innocent customers), an alluvial diggings on the Lachlan. Lambing Flats was without any public hall or other place suitable for show purposes; and I had given up all idea of a performance, when I was approached by a Jew named Cohen, who declared himself "an Amerigan citsin" and offered me the use of his large wagon shed provided I would remove and replace about six tons of pumpkins that were stored there. This business consumed some three hours for each process, but the box receipts warranted the labor.

Our next stop was at Wombat, a little village where it was the custom to send a crier about the surrounding farms to announce the advent of any shows, meetings, or other matters of importance, a device which usually resulted in large gatherings. Unfortunately for us, although the old bell-ringer performed his duty faithfully, fear of bushrangers, road agents, and cattle duffers, who were then operating extensively in that neighborhood, kept the people at home, and we just managed to pay expenses.

While we were some seven or eight miles from Wombat *en route* to Molong, the weather being exceedingly hot, the wheels began to squeak—a not uncommon occurrence during the summer months—and I drove into a water-hole to soak them. The horses were unhitched, and we took shelter from the sun in a grove nearby. As I was suffering from a bad headache, I wandered away from the rest into the scrub. Walking through a dense clump of saplings, I tripped over some large body and fell headlong. On picking myself up I discovered that the impediment to my progress was the corpse of a large man lying face down with the hands tied tightly behind his back and his feet tied to a tree. On turning the body over I saw that the throat was cut from ear to ear. I immediately forgot my headache and, hastening back to my family, jumped on one of the horses and posted back to Wombat to inform the police. Two troopers were immediately detailed to accompany me to the scene of the crime. As the only conveyances allowed the police in those days were light two-wheeled spring carts, the three of us rode back together, leading the horse. According to the police regulations then in use, it was a rule to remove all bodies found out of doors to the nearest private or public house, to which the coroner was called to sit. This body was taken to the Wombat hotel and the inquest ordered for the following day. As I did not wish to remain, I was allowed to make a sworn deposition which excused me from appearing; and I continued my journey. Some days later I saw a newspaper report of the inquest, stating that a verdict of suicide had been rendered. This was not surprising: it was then customary to avoid the trouble and expense incurred by a verdict of murder by construing as suicides every possible case, and some impossible ones. In this instance, however, the razor with which the deed was committed was found some hundred yards from the corpse, and one of the jury asked how, in a case of suicide, it could have got so far away. This problem was immediately settled by an old bushman who gave his opinion that it had been carried there by an iguana, a large lizard some ten or twelve feet in length, much sought on account of a penetrating medicinal oil which is found in its head, sometimes to the quantity of a pint. This ridiculous verdict appealed so insistently to my sense of humor that I finally drew a little sketch of the scene, in which the captive was shown tied hand and foot while an iguana climbed a tree with a large American axe in his mouth. I sent this to the police at Wombat, where it was posted in the station, much to the amusement of all who saw it.

A few miles beyond the scene of the murder we stopped to water our horses at a wine shanty, as the disreputable little road inns were called. Here we were accosted by a tough-looking crowd of young boundary riders and cattle duffers who were playing quoits in the yard. They tried to induce me to join the game, but, finding me resolved to continue my journey, they began to jeer and make very unedifying remarks as to my profession, ancestry, and destination, much to the delight of the pockmarked landlord and his blowsy wife. As we drove away they shouted after us: "Never mind! We'll overhaul you before you get far!"

As the weather was frightfully hot and the horses exhausted, all thought of reaching Molong that night had to be abandoned; and about five o'clock the party made camp in a little wood a short distance back from the creek. With my wife and children I occupied the tent, while our two men and young Carney (my brother-in-law, who was now one of the family) slept a short distance away under a tree near the coach. The combined funds of the whole party were put in a tin bucket, which was hung under the coach, that being the place into which robbers would be least likely to peer in quest of it—for we were all more or less disturbed by the remarks of the quoit players.

About two o'clock in the morning we were awakened by the trampling of horses, yelling of men, and firing of pistols. We were hardly on our feet before four of the larrikins were in our midst. The leader shouted for the gaffer, saying: "Don't be scared. We don't want to hurt you. All we want is L.S.D." The marauders were all drunk, but, born to the saddle, they could stick to a horse when unable to walk. On being told that the outfit was broke, one of them reeled off his horse, staggered to the wagon, and, putting his hand into the bucket, pulled out a pair of new hobbles which were lying on top of the money, saying: "Thanks! We'll leave these at Molong for you." With some difficulty and much cursing he remounted, and with an unearthly yell the quartette put spurs to their horses and galloped away, the sound of their retreat falling like sweet music on our ears.

As sleep was no longer possible, we made an early start. About noon we reached a neat little inn, where we stopped for lunch. Although the whole hostelry consisted of but two rooms, only one of which was for public use, the exceptional tidiness of the place was most attractive and a marked contrast to the usual filth of the road-houses which abounded in that territory. There was no bar, but several rows of neatly labelled and shining bottles were arranged on shelves fastened to the wall; the floor was merely of hard-pressed earth, but it was covered by several mats of kangaroo and emu skin; and the furniture consisted of three homemade benches and a table. On the wall was a large slate on which was written, "Please talk to us on the slate." Both the worthy landlord and his wife were deaf and dumb! Carney, who was an adept at talking with his hands, conversed with the old lady while I utilized the slate for the benefit of the old man. All this resulted in an excellent meal. After it the journey was continued to Molong, which we reached that night, but too late for a performance.

On interviewing the village publican the following morning, I learned that arrangements were being made to hold a church fair that evening in the only available hall, which was also the church and schoolhouse; and it was suggested that the minister be interviewed on the subject of allowing the panorama entertainment to become a part of the bazaar. Accordingly, the obliging landlord piloted me to the parsonage and introduced me to the clergyman. This expounder of the gospel was a little round-shouldered man in a clerical coat many sizes too large, wearing a much frayed and soiled collar with the necktie under one ear. He was seated on the head of a barrel marked "New York dried apples," with a black T.D. pipe between his clean-shaven lips; and he was in a very inebriated condition. However, he was exceedingly amiable, and he warmly approved the idea of a joint performance. Handbills, or "dodgers," as the vernacular had it, were given for distribution to the bell-ringer, who was also baker, undertaker, fireman, and local poet; the panorama was erected at the end of the low, stageless hall; and the ladies of the church decorated and arranged their tables. As the opening hour approached, the crowd began to gather, coming in wagon loads from far and near, until the house was packed and many were endeavoring to look in through the doors and windows. The panorama entertainment was given first. Then the local poet, bell-ringer, etc., recited an original production concocted for the occasion, in which were many local hits that pleased the audience immensely. The evening ended with a round of old-fashioned dances, for which I furnished the music. As I pumped away at the old concertina, white stockings, pantalettes, and prunella shoes flew about in unison with riding boots and spurs, as the happy crowd stepped on one another's toes in the mazes of the mazurka and other dances of the period.

The next morning, everything being packed, we bade farewell to our religious collaborators and started away on our long trip for Victoria, many miles away. The weather was frightfully hot, and the numerous heavy thunderstorms of the past week had rendered the roads almost impassable. In truth, there was no road at all, in the accepted sense of the word. There was only a rough cart-path trailing through the bush and containing innumerable mudholes. For one stretch of about six miles, it ran along the sides of the foothills of a range of volcanic mountains at so abrupt an angle that there was constant danger of capsizing the coach into the shallow, muddy-bottomed Molong Creek. On certain parts of this dangerous trail it was necessary for all to leave the coach. While Mrs. Peirce and the children walked behind, the men, fastening a rope about the coach body, moved along the upper side and hauled lustily to keep it from tipping over, while I remained on the box to guide the slipping, sliding horses. After some three hours of this strenuous travelling we came out upon low, flat ground which merged into sand along the bank of the creek; and, much tired from our unwonted exertions, we decided to make camp for the night.

In the morning we found that one of our horses, though hobbled, had learned like many others to run rabbit-fashion despite the restraint, and was now hopping along the creek bank at a rapid pace. We immediately chased him into the creek, where he became imbedded in the mud and refused to move. All attempts to extricate him proved futile, for he utterly declined to assist in any way. Finally, in despair and anger, I cried "We'll have to kill him. Get the axe!" To our amazement he seemed to understand the words: he immediately began to flounder and was soon pulled out and put in harness.

Two days later, after a hard journey over wretched roads, we reached Orange, a familiar place to us. But we had shown here so many times that we were no longer a drawing attraction; and, just managing to pay expenses, we moved on through Tarcutta, Three Mile, and Adelong to Wagga Wagga, which we entered on New Year's Day of 1876. At this time Wagga Wagga was entirely controlled by the Masons, and no one who was not a member of that order could do any business in the town without being subject to boycott. On learning that I was a brother, the whole population became interested in my performance. We opened to a packed house, which continued during our short stay.

One day I happened to remark to Mr. Cox, landlord of *The Australian*, where we were staying, that I was tired of the show business and desired to return to the river; whereupon that worthy man informed me that he was a large owner in the Murrumbidgee Steam Navigation Company, and that the *Victoria*, a large boat belonging to that corporation, was then lying at Echuca undergoing repairs and without a commander. He expressed a wish that I might have the position. He accordingly introduced me to Shaw & Edmunds, a Wagga Wagga firm which was managing the line; and my reputation as a navigator, together with Mr. Cox's influence, resulted in my engagement as commander, with orders to repair at once to Echuca and prepare the *Victoria* for the season's work.

Two days later, in excellent spirits at the bright prospect of my again commanding on the river, and with my signed commission in my pocket, we drove out of Wagga Wagga *en route* for Echuca. A few miles before reaching Albury, while trotting along at a good rate, I caught sight, among the bushes by the roadside, of the crown of a cabbage-tree hat like those manufactured by the convicts at Parramatta. I was soon able to distinguish the figure of a man seated on a lathered horse, apparently lurking in ambush. Young Carney, who was on the box with me, also saw the highwayman and in childish bravado hastily grasped an old property pistol lying on the seat and, jumping on the top of the coach just as we came up to the outlaw, levelled it at the fellow's head and yelled to him to give himself up. At the same instant three other riders came up from opposite directions and bailed up the coach. Knowing that there were several bands of bushrangers then operating in that district, among them the famous Clarke and Moonlight gangs, I was well aware that resistance was worse than useless; and I decided to be as civil to my detainers as possible, readily answering all their questions as to my name, business, and destination. Satisfied on this score, they apologized for stopping me, saying that they had mistaken us for the mail coach, which was due about this time; and, having taken a bottle of wine (for which they offered to pay), and having warned me to say nothing should I meet any troopers, they allowed us to pass on without further molestation. A few hours later we were passing into Albury, by the old gum tree which bore the tablet in honor of Hume, the discoverer of the great Murray River, which, together with the town of Albury, once bore his name. (As this tree was enclosed by an iron fence, many people got the erroneous idea that the explorer was buried there.)

Early the following morning we crossed over to Wodonga on the opposite shore and plodded along over country very familiar to me, although many changes had occurred during my absence—among them the great improvement which we noticed in the road. Ledges had been blasted, hills graded, culverts built, and a breakwater constructed to keep back the floods, which had always perpetrated damage yearly when the river rose. But all these improvements were wiped away the following heavy season, and the road was impassable for months save by boats. Then it was more securely reconstructed and brought to its present condition.

We passed through Beechworth and Wangaratta, journeying across the country later so famous for the desperate scenes of the Kelly Brothers' operations, to Peechebla; thence across the Goulburn by Stuart's old draw-bridge, so noted as the lurking place of many desperate characters (for nearly a quarter of a century it had borne a placard marked "dangerous!" warning all passers that they crossed it at their own risk); thence into the great lumber country just north of Echuca. We camped on a little rise at a bend in the river a few miles outside the town, opposite Boil-O, so called from its large rendering establishment. Thousands of sheep, after the shearing, when the market is too low to pay their transportation to

Melbourne, are put in sweat-rooms to scald off the short wool and afterward boiled down for tallow, the tongues being preserved for exportation and domestic use.

The next morning I was awakened by the puffing of a steamer. On going down to the water's edge I saw coming round the bend one of the little boats that tow barges of logs from the saw-mills of Echuca. I was delighted to recognize in her captain my old mate Samuel Williams. He was greatly surprised to see me, for the rumor of my death had been in circulation for some months. On hearing that I was going to command the *Victoria* he thought there must be some mistake, for that berth had been given to James Austin a few days before by McCulloch & Company, the Echuca agents of the Navigation Company. I hastened down to their office and showed my commission. It displeased them very much; but they settled the matter by appointing Austin first mate.

I immediately inspected the boat, and, with the advice of the port surveyor, Frederick Bigbee, formerly engineer of the British Navy, turned her boiler and changed the coal bunkers, which had sunk the bow much below the stem. I soon had her on an even keel. A week or so later the *Victoria*, scraped and painted and in excellent condition, was lying with her cargo aboard awaiting the rise of the river; and soon afterward she was puffing upstream, the first boat of the season.

As far as the mouth of the Wakool, the Murrumbidgee was familiar, and I experienced no difficulty in moving rapidly up stream, although the river was unusually high and overflowing its banks, being a regular "banker," as the river men say. Beyond the junction all was mystery, for no information could be obtained as to the condition of the river. The first stop was made at Cannally station, owned by John Maguire, a native of Boston, who, having been withdrawn from the Constantinople consulate during the Pierce administration, was appointed consul at Melbourne by Buchanan. When relieved from this post by the succeeding administration, he decided to take up his permanent residence in Australia. He established the great sheep and cattle ranch at Cannally, where he built a fine mansion after the style of the old Virginia plantation homes. Here a large quantity of supplies was sold and a freight contract made for carrying the season's wool down on the return trip.

Similar transactions were gone through with at the next station, Boroga, which had acquired much notoriety as the first to introduce American sheep—a complete failure owing to the inferior quality of the wool, which was much coarser than that of the Australian cross-bred.

The first settlement encountered was the little village of Balranald. Here considerable consigned cargo was left, a large portion of which was destined for various stations back along the unnavigable bed of the Lachlan. Among these was the Ivanhoe, the noted station of Tyson, one of the wealthiest of all Australian ranch owners.

Although the river was uncharted and unknown to me and I had nothing upon which to depend for the detection of reefs and snags save the ripples and general appearance of the water, it was important to keep well ahead of the following boats of rival companies. So I pushed the *Victoria* up river night and day to Hay, the largest and most important river port on the Murrumbidgee. Here the steamer was boarded by a pompous and fussy little customs officer, more bedizened with gold lace than a Turkish admiral, who, having examined the papers and minutely inspected the cargo, allowed its removal. This was a most disagreeable job for the crew, who, no stevedores being found, were obliged to carry a great number of large sheets of corrugated iron ashore on their heads under a burning sun. To all appearances, about everyone in the town had been celebrating the expected arrival of the first boat with so much enthusiasm and energy that all were in various stages of inebriation. In fact, one of the police troopers asserted that he had been watching one man who seemed suspiciously sober, and had found the motive for his sobriety in an attempt to purloin a quantity of spokes and wheels from the local blacksmith shop, for which the straight-laced old Scotch "beak" (a polite term for magistrate) had just sent him to durance vile for thirty days.

The trip from Hay, which is about half-way between Echuca and Wagga Wagga, was almost without incident. It was, however, most successful from a financial point of view; for large sales were made at all the stations, and contracts were signed for the carriage of wool on the return trip. Among the points touched were several stations of the Burrabogie Company (but, as they operated steamers of their own, only a few small sales were made); two stations owned by the Rutherfords, who also had extensive holdings along the upper Murray; Deepwater, belonging to Devlin Brothers, of interest to the naturalist from the remarkable appearance of a solitary and immense rock which rears to a height of some eighty feet in an open plain of sandy formation, and also as the abode of that extremely rare species of kangaroo which is white and pink-eyed; Gangmain, where the river was full of boulders, on two or three of which the *Victoria* struck, fortunately without damage; and Naranda and Gillenbah, formerly the haunt of Morgan and kindred spirits.

Finally, after a most successful trip, we reached Wagga Wagga in fourteen days—an unprecedented passage, the speed of which was accounted for by the readiness with which the steamer answered her helm since the change in the position of the boiler. A large and enthusiastic crowd was at the wharf awaiting us, and so pleased was it at our unexpectedly early arrival that when I came ashore to make my report I was immediately seized and lifted on the shoulders of some of the largest and carried in this manner to the company's office. We remained five days taking on cargo, and then started back on the return trip. As I had made a chart of the river on the upward passage, I was now perfectly confident of my ability to avoid all obstacles; and the trip down was rapidly accomplished. Five successful trips were made this season before the fall of the river necessitated putting the boat out of commission.

It was during this season that great excitement was created along the Murrumbidgee and through the surrounding country by the news that a Wagga Wagga butcher named Castro had proclaimed himself the baronet Sir Roger Tichborne and had induced several of the townspeople, among whom Peter MacAllister was the heaviest subscriber, to advance enough money to enable him to return to England to claim his inheritance. It is needless here to go into the details of this celebrated case, —it gained world-wide renown,—but it may be of interest to state that the people of Wagga Wagga thoroughly believed in his cause and were indignant at his treatment. The wretched little hut where he had killed his meat and where his common Irish wife had done the *Victoria's* laundry, was torn to pieces for souvenirs of him, and on its site was erected a fine block of stone buildings, called Tichborne Block in honor of the "butcher baronet."

11

JUST before the following season opened, Edward Barnes, master of the *Riverina*, who had been my mate on the *Lady Daly*, resigned his command to take charge of the Albury Company's new steamer *Cumberrona*, and the *Riverina* was offered to me. Although she was a small, low-water boat, very inferior in appearance to the *Victoria*, I accepted the command; for the salary was much larger, and she was to run the year round. I held command of this boat for about a year, during which time I added greatly to my knowledge concerning the aborigines; for I was in almost daily contact with the Murrumbidgee blacks.

The tribes in this locality are very inferior to those in Queensland, whence come most of the black troopers and native police trackers. They are small in stature, with thick wavy hair, flat features, and exceedingly black skins. Although by nature they are nomadic and wander about the country in any direction, attracted by prospects of food, they carry no shelters or utensils, as do the American Indians, but either sleep out under the sky, lying in circular groups with their feet to little fires, or else build temporary huts of bark called *mia-mias*, which are constructed simply by driving two forked sticks into the ground to support a rail against which boughs and sheets of bark are laid. When they have found good fishing or hunting grounds where they desire to remain for any length of time, they construct a more permanent shelter called a *gunyah*. This also is made of bark; it has three walls and a roof, and is open on one side, which, is closed in rainy weather by laying sheets of bark against it. Some portions of the river banks are lined with little villages of these *gunyahs*, crowded with filthy natives and mangy mongrel dogs—the latter generally hairless, owing to their habit of sleeping in warm ashes.

No clothing whatever is worn except during the wet seasons, when possum-skin rugs are sometimes thrown about the shoulders. They plant no crops but live entirely on what lies nearest at hand, fish being the principal article of food, with wild fowl, kangaroo, opossum, wombat, paddymelon, bandicoot, eggs, and nardoo (a little shell bean similar to a beech-nut). Some tribes eat snakes, although most natives are very much afraid of them.

Much ingenuity is shown in their unique methods of hunting. They stretch large meshed nets between the upper branches of trees across the lower end of a lagoon, and, while some go to the other end of the water to beat up the game by running, yelling, and waving their arms, thus starting the ducks across the water, others remain behind the net and throw boomerangs at the approaching game. The boomerangs so confuse them that they drop into the nets and quickly become entangled. Another practice is to cover the back of the neck with reeds, in which disguise they wade and crawl out into the marshes, imitating perfectly the noise of ducks. On the approach of the actual ducks they quickly reach out under water and, catching the legs, drag them in and immediately wring their necks. In hunting the emu, they cover themselves with emu skins and, holding an arm and hand in the air to resemble the neck and head of the bird, are able to get very near their unsuspecting victims.

The culinary methods in use among all tribes are the simplest imaginable. The recipe for game is merely to take the bird *au naturel, cover* it thickly with clay, and throw it into a bed of coals, where it roasts until the clay cracks. Then it is withdrawn and the covering is stripped off, taking all the feathers with it. On its being opened, the entrails are found shrunk into a little ball; this is quickly removed. A fish is treated in much the same way except that, instead of laying it in the coals, they thrust a stick through the eyes and suspend it over the fire. For vegetables, they dig up yams with pointed yam-sticks and make a flour of manna, a white substance that exudes from the leaves of the manna trees. All these are seasoned with branches of salt bush which they chew; for, although the country abounds in salt pans, of which there are thousands of acres, they never use them.

They are very adept in curing skins. These they peg down on the earth to allow the sun to boil out the fat. Then the skins are rubbed in ashes, which cleanses them perfectly. After this, dry and clean, they are tied in packs and taken into the townships for sale. If the tribe happens to be travelling during the curing process, the pelts are attached to strips of bark and tied to the backs of the women, who always act as beasts of burden for whatever dunnage is carried about. In fact, as among all other savages, the women do all the work that is done, cooking the food, sewing pelts into rugs with kangaroo sinews, and building the huts, while the men hunt, fish, and loaf.

So far as I could observe from my long acquaintance with them, extending over thirty years in different parts of the continent, they are utterly ignorant of such a thing as a marriage ceremony. The people mate as suits their fancy, granted the approval of their leaders. Although they often treat their women with brutality, they have a certain sense of property rights which makes them extremely jealous of their *leubras,* although they will lend them to their friends or sell their favors to the whites—this last being considered quite an honor.

They also seem to be devoid of any ideas of a religious significance, except that they are in deadly fear of the evil spirit which they call "Borree." One may travel the country over and never find any idols or other paraphernalia of religion. Even the medicine man is less a priest than a physician and undertaker. It is he who prescribes for their sickness and embalms the bodies of their kings, using herbs the selection and preparation of which he alone knows. Either to propitiate or to frighten the Borree—and it is impossible for a white man to become so far initiated into the aboriginal mysteries as to discover which—at the time of the full moon all the men of the tribe retire to a secluded place, erect a pole to which a piece, of bark is attached, and as they dance about this pole, yelling, and gesticulating, whirl the bark, which gives out wild shrieks and squawks as it rubs against the pole. In the meantime the women and children, who have been left in the village in supposed ignorance of the object of the males' absence, collect in a group and pound possum rugs and yell with all their might so as to drown any sound of the male contingent's ceremonies which might otherwise reach them; for it is believed that if the women hear the noise raised by the men the Borree will pounce down and instantly dispatch them. As such a massacre has never been known to occur, the female aboriginal eardrums must be of much coarser material than those of the white race, for it is impossible on a clear night to avoid hearing the racket produced by the men at a distance of ten miles from the scene.

Even the funeral rites seem void of religious significance so far as an outsider can judge—although it has been asserted by some travellers that they show faint signs of belief in the power of the spirits of the dead; a belief which tends toward ancestor-worship. The various tribes of different localities have different methods of disposing of their dead, just as they have different dialects, members of one tribe being incapable of understanding or conversing with one another. Along the Murrumbidgee it is customary to dig shallow graves about two feet in depth and just sufficiently large to admit the body, which is then thrown in without any covering. The dirt is then heaped up and covered with a few strips of bark. These are held down by two or three large rocks, either to protect the grave or to prevent the rising of its tenant—for all aborigines are mortally afraid of their deceased. In marshy country, scaffolds are erected on which the body is left to the sun and crows. Near the Murray, a widow shaves her head with shells and broken bottles, covers it with netting, and plasters it with human excrement which, when dried, forms a sort of skull cap from an inch to several inches in thickness; but in general no mourning is observed.

By temperament the blacks are not naturally warlike, and the tribal conflicts are generally contemptible. Large masses of warriors expend their powers in yelling and gesticulating to frighten their adversaries, rather than in doing them bodily harm. Usually, after an all-day battle, the casualties average only about five wounded. However, they have special implements of war, which are entirely distinct from those used for hunting. For the former is reserved the *nulla-nulla* or *waddy*, which is merely a stout stick of ironwood some three feet long and terminating in a large knob. The spear and boomerang are used for hunting, as is also a curious instrument called by the whites a tangle-foot; it consists of a wooden handle some two feet long, to one end of which is attached by a cord a wooden ball about an inch in diameter. This is mostly employed in emu hunting. It is thrown with great precision and skill about the legs of the victim, entangling them and making escape hopeless.

Like all savages, the Australians are not without their games, although these require little or no skill and are of a most infantile nature. The most popular amusement is to play with the *witchie-witchie*, which is nothing more than a cigar-shaped piece of wood to which is attached a red tail of rope. It is so flung as to hop along the ground for from sixty to eighty yards, at which they set up a great laugh and chatter.

They also have dances for numerous occasions; but these, though slightly varied, are all fundamentally similar. The skeleton dance, already described, and the monkey or kangaroo dance are the most distinctive. In the latter, which usually takes place around the funeral pyre of a monarch, the males wear belts to which are attached tails of kangaroo grass three or four feet in length and some two inches in diameter. Having formed a circle, they get down on all fours and run about the pyre, pulling one another's tails, leaping over each other's backs, and performing various antics of a similar nature, during the whole time keeping up this continuous and monotonous chant in a bass voice: "Ging-bar! Ging-bar! Ogle lara-bar! Yong dol bungalar! Bingle catha roga! Kin-gar, lara-gar!" which is repeated by the women in shrill falsetto.

The blacks are very keen woodsmen and are well informed in wood-craft, for which they show wonderful aptitude. They can generally predict rain by the appearance of the leaves of the eucalyptus tree and by the sound of the fallen leaves, which often give before a storm a cracking sound due to some atmospheric influence. Their sense of hearing is very acute, and by lying with an ear on the ground near a river bank they will foretell the approach of a steamer from twenty miles away and state its direction. Also, by the same means they can accurately foretell the approach of a mounted party at ten miles' distance, even enumerating the party and knowing when its members stop or dismount. Yet all the time the woods about them are ringing with the cries of birds, which, to white ears, drown all other sounds. Their great ability and trustworthiness in this respect are so well recognized that the government has used them to advantage in tracking outlaws.

In personal adornment, so popular among most savage tribes as well as civilized communities, the Australian has little interest. Tattooing is unknown among them. In some tribes the women, on reaching the age of puberty, scarify their breasts with three parallel bars just above the nipples, and also raise on the upper parts of their arms scars similar to chevrons; and the men are obliged to suffer the knock- ing-out of two front teeth. Both sexes usually have the septum of the nose bored for the insertion of an ornamental fish bone. The unfortunate male babies of the Adelaide blacks are covered at birth with a soft, fine hair, which as they grow older it is customary to pluck out as one would pluck a chicken—a most painful operation.

All the aborigines are great drunkards and have made from time immemorial a fermented liquor from the nadoo bean. (This has, however, been rapidly displaced by the distilled liquors of the whites.) Their fond-ness for intoxicants is so great that they are ready to part with all their belongings for a dram; and a very heavy fine has been imposed for barter-ing their government supplies away from them with liquor. That they are not particular as to the purity of their drinks is illustrated by the following incident: The *Lady Daly* was once discharging a cargo of English ale at Wentworth by black stevedores, when one of the barrels was dropped into the barge and broken. Thereupon the whole concourse of natives dropped into the barge and drank it all up, even to lapping up the bilge water and licking, the planks; and finally they attacked the hops, which they chewed and swallowed.

12

HAVING completed a year's command of the *Riverina*, I was offered a new opening. A bright American, Frank Ellwood Jackson, had conceived a new idea in the advertising business which he intended to introduce all over the continent. It was his practice to canvass a whole town, solicit business cards for a few pounds each, and then have an artist make sketches of the shops and stores of the subscribers. These drawings, with the accompanying advertising matter, were lithographed and produced in sheets, to be placarded about the town in conspicuous places and hung up in the hotel offices and other public resorts. Having seen some of my work, he visited me at Moama and offered me a salary of such ample proportions that I resigned my position and left steamboating, never to return.

As Jackson was established at Adelaide, I set out for that place *via* Melbourne, whence I sailed again on the old *Korong* under Captain William McLean, whose sudden death shortly afterward, while he was witnessing a performance at the Theatre Royal in Melbourne, was a great loss to the coasting interests. He had come to Melbourne as master of the large side-wheeler excursion boat *Hygeia*, which he had brought out from Great Britain to be used on Hobson's Bay; and he had been engaged for many years in the coasting trade between Adelaide and Melbourne, where he had won the regard and respect of all who knew him.

Arriving at Adelaide, I went at once to the Imperial Hotel, whose host was generally known as *The Flycatcher*, from his enormous and usually open mouth. Here we made our headquarters. The advertising project was well received, and large numbers of subscribers kept me busy for many weeks from morning until night making sketches of their establishments.

Then we went to Kapunda, in the great copper-mining district some thirty miles distant, and drew some of the large smelting works. We also went to Burra Burra, so named because the miners . dwelt in dugouts exca-vated in the sides of the hills, many of which can still be seen, although the copper mines, discovered in 1843, have now run out, owing to the filling of the pits by numerous natural springs which made the expense of mining too great to be profitable. Visits of a like nature were made to Jamestown and Gladstone. At the latter place we saw many gangs of convicts "knapping diamonds" for the government roads. This process is merely the breaking into small pieces of a lustrous metallic blue stone which abounds in this region. It is done with a short iron hammer having a long and flexible hickory handle. Others besides prisoners engage in this work. It is paid for by the cubic yard; the government inspectors survey each pile, using a certain size of iron ring, and if they discover one piece too large to pass through this ring they condemn the whole pile. They also carry iron rods with which they prod the heaps, for the laborers are much given to hiding large unbroken pieces at the center.

From Gladstone we proceeded to Clare (a beautiful little town noted for its large breweries), Port Augusta, Ardolf, Milang, Goolwa, and all the places of any importance in Adelaide, consuming some six months in a most profitable business.

During our stay in the city of Adelaide, I added to my income by furnishing weekly cartoons to *The Lantern,* Carroll's comic weekly. One drawing created much attention: it was a caricature of one of the country members of parliament who was strongly advocating a measure for the extermination of rabbits, proposing that the government can and place them on the market. An English gentleman, editor and owner of another paper of the same sort, wishing to leave the country, sold out his rights to us; and Jackson and Pierce thus became the proprietors of *The Figaro.* As I now devoted all my humor to my own paper, Carroll became much disgusted with our success and published many disagreeable insinuations about my character and ability. I retaliated, and war was declared. As Carroll was then standing for parliament, *The Figaro* wrought his down-fall by publishing a true story of the candidate's previous career in New Zealand, where he had operated as a forger under various aliases and served terms for the same. On leaving the city we sold out this paper to our printer.

Having completed the tour of Adelaide, we went to Melbourne, where we conducted the same business with great success for some four or five months. Then another tour was made through Beechworth, Ballarat, Maryborough, Clunes, Backcreek, Lamplough, Dunolly, and Ararat, including all the important mining and agricultural districts. Then we returned to Melbourne, and Jackson devised a new advertising scheme. He made a contract with the railroads by which he was allowed to put an attractive advertising frame in every station along the lines for ten pounds each. The frames were about three by four feet; they had a mirror in the center, a thermometer on one side, and a barometer on the other, and they were surmounted by a clock. They attracted much attention, and consequently no trouble was found in disposing of the advertising space at high prices. Melbourne was successfully recanvassed, the idea was introduced most satisfactorily at Sydney, and a trip was made to Perth and Freemantle on the Swan River in Western Australia (a locality noted for a hard and soapy red gum called Swan River mahogany which is extensively used in the sheathing of vessels).

Here I parted with Jackson, who left Australia for India to carry on the same business there, with the understanding that I was to join him at Bombay if the prospect seemed to warrant it. But this was the last I ever saw of him, and years afterward I learned that he had met his death in an Indian tiger hunt. After waiting some weeks without hearing from him, I left Perth and went to Geelong. There I became acquainted with a wealthy man named William Bignell, who, having just returned from England filled with the idea of advertising Australia in the old country, wanted a panorama showing the customs of the aborigines, views of the fine agricultural districts, scenes of the best sheep runs and cattle stations, and illustrations of the great gold fields. It was his intention to carry this to England and, by touring Great Britain and Ireland, encourage immigration to the Australian colonies. He hoped to be reimbursed for his expenditure by the Victorian government.

He engaged me to paint the scenes; and a year later, in 1880, the work was finished. It comprised some twenty-four nine-by-twelve-foot canvases. But Bignell was greatly disappointed by the refusal of the government to subsidize his enterprise, and he abandoned all thought of the British tour.

Instead he decided to make a trip through the colonies. He engaged as a star attraction, at fifty pounds a week, De Lacy Evans, the woman miner who had successfully disguised her sex for so many years in the gold fields. We opened to an exceptionally good house in Geelong, where we drew great crowds nightly for three weeks. But the rest of the trip hardly paid expenses, and the project was abandoned after a four months' trial.

Tired of continuous travelling, I decided to settle down for a while in Geelong. Thither I moved my family and, opening a studio, devoted myself to art for some ten years. I did not, however, confine myself exclusively to my studio work. I engaged in several outside interests—operating the "Geelong Cigar Divan" on Coria Street for a year or so with fair success (although the profits were not so great as the business seemed to warrant, owing to the heavy duty on tobacco, all of which was imported, the native product being fit only for fumigation and sheep washing); managing the Black Bull Hotel, a celebrated professional house, for some fifteen months; and acting as head scene- painter for the Geelong Exhibition Theatre, in which I had a financial interest.

About the second year of my stay at Geelong, I was surprised by a hurried and excited call of my old friend Joseph Nash, a reporter on the Melbourne *Age*, who informed me that the notorious Kelly Brothers had been captured at Greta and that he was going up to investigate and write up the affair. He asked me to go with him and make the sketches.

The Kelly boys and their companions—well-known outlaws all of whom had prices on their heads dead or alive, among them Byrnes and Sherritt—had swooped down on Greta the day before and, having bailed up the town and torn up the railroad, proceeded to gather the principal townspeople into Jones's Hotel and make merry. Word, however, was sent to the police; and a large body of troopers came up, surrounded the house, and demanded the surrender of the outlaws. On their refusal the police shot into the house, and the Kellys returned the fire. Then the Greta priest appeared at the door and informed the police that if they would with-hold fire the Kellys would allow the townspeople to leave the premises. This was done, and a second demand of surrender made. But the Kellys refused to move, and the police were at a loss what to do. They contem-plated burning the house, and even sent to Melbourne for a cannon to blow it down. Finally they charged the place, firing heavy volleys into the house as they advanced. Receiving no answer, they broke in and found the outlaws dead or dying—all of them except Ned Kelly, their leader, who had disappeared. Early the following morning he was discovered by Troopers Arthur and Steele, who were watching in the fog. They saw something of gigantic size rise in the mist and move away. Taking no chances, they fired. The object returned the fire and then fell; whereupon they rushed upon it and found it to be Ned Kelly, dressed in a full armor of ploughshares, later found to weigh some two hundred pounds.

We arrived just after Kelly was taken and witnesses the placing of the dead bodies of the outlaws in the courtyard to be photographed. Ned Kelly was taken to Melbourne, where his trial was the sensation of the time. After it I saw him hanged; on the scaffold he turned coward.

Soon after this experience I engaged in a few theatrical adventures, accompanying one of Charles McMann's companies to Hobart, Tasmania. It is noted for the peculiar appearance of Mount Wellington, at whose foot it lies. This mountain seems to rise like an immense organ, the deep furrows wrought in its face by snow and water suggesting mighty organ pipes. I also acted as stage manager for a company presenting the burlesque of *Bluebeard* at Ballarat and Bendigo; and I visited the same places shortly afterward in the same capacity with a legitimate drama company of which the leading man was John Sheridan, an American actor, and the leading lady the celebrated and much regretted Fanny Davenport.

About this time Neil Burgess, an American actor, under the management of Charles McMann, appeared at the "Exposition" with his famous play *The County Fair*, in which occurs the well-remembered horse-race scene. This necessitated cutting up the whole stage; and, although every night of his stay resulted in a crowded and overflowing house, yet on his departure the expense involved in returning the stage to its former condition was so great as to cause the proprietors' assignment and succession by William Somers.

During this ten-year stay in Geelong I painted, among other productions, animal portraits of James Wilson's celebrated stallion cup winner, King of the Ring (this was presented by the owner to the Victoria Racing Club, where it now hangs in the stewards' room), Frisco King, Progress, Malvolio,—all well-known turf favorites,—and James Russell's famous ten-thousand-pound ram, Merino.

In 1891 the great boom in Victoria lands came, bringing with it an inflated prosperity to all business; and I, like many of my friends and neighbors, saw large prospects before me in commerce. Having an opportunity to purchase the Rose of Australia, a flourishing hotel near the great Metropolitan Meat Market at Melbourne, I bade farewell to Geelong and entered on my new occupation with great hopes. After six months of most profitable business the great boom burst, followed by the depression, with its accompanying strikes and riots, which usually succeeds an unnatural prosperity. The great market and the foundry of Yard & Crystal nearby both closed their doors, and I again went out of business.

I opened a new studio and devoted my attention to painting once more. It was at this time that the celebrated murder case of Maria Needles was stirring Melbourne. This woman, the keeper of a lodging-house in that city, was arrested on the charge of poisoning one of her lodgers, a young German. The peculiar deaths of her husband and three children some time previously led Detective Whitney, who was working on the case, to suspect that they also might have met with foul play, and he got permission to exhume and examine the bodies. As he was a friend of mine, he engaged me to accompany him and make sketches of the scene. One cold, foggy, disagreeable morning of July, we, together with the coroner, drove out to the place of disinterment, and the disagreeable task was carried out. Despite the neatly-cared-for graves and handsome tombstones bearing the most affectionate epitaphs, enough poison was discovered in the stomachs of the father and three children to have caused the deaths of a hundred persons. Martha Needle paid the penalty on the scaffold at Melbourne jail, where I witnessed her execution.

On the death of my wife in 1894, my thoughts turned to my old home in my native land. The wish to return to America, visit my family, and see the friends of my youth became very strong. Despite the fact that I had already got as far as Perth on my way to the new gold fields of Western Australia, a letter from my relatives in New England made my longing so irresistible that I turned back and, hastening through Melbourne to Sydney, engaged passage on the *Wyomorah* for Vancouver.

As the *Wyomorah* steamed away I took my last look at the fast-receding shores of the adoptive country where over thirty years of my life had been spent. They finally disappeared; and I turned my face to the east, toward the land of my birth and the home of my ancestors, where my brothers and sister were waiting to welcome my return.

TIMELINE

1840

Augustus Baker Peirce born to Major Moses Peirce and his wife Mehitable Nye on October 7 in West Medford, Massachusetts, USA.

1859

Sailor on the *Oriental* under Captain Osgood.

1860

Peirce deserted the *Oriental* at Port Philip in January, swimming ashore. Painted 'No Smoking' signs for Cobb & Co, sold pies for George Millbank at New Inglewood, Wizard Oil for Frank Weston at Dunolly.

1861

Photographer's assistant with Batchelder & O'Neil (of Salem Massechusetts) in Bendigo, while being instructed in scene painting by John Fry at the Lyceum Theatre. Painted scenes for the Theatre Royal at Castlemaine, and a 24 foot long canvas for the Dunolly Hotel and two scenes for Ellis's Hotel, Tarrengower.

The *Lady Daly* at Mannum, with Captain Gus Pierce (top right).

The *Jane Eliza.*

1862

Pierce violently assaulted by Gion Pininula at Inglewood. Hunting for snakes with Joe Shires, inventor of a snake-bite cure. Meets John Egge at Wentworth, NSW, where he acts as a bum-bailiff in his case against a family of acrobats. Went to New Zealand as a sailor on the *Ottago* for the gold rush, and returned on the steamer *You-Yangs* to Melbourne.

1863

In January he worked again for Batchelder in Bendigo, and accompanied the amateur photographer John Creelman, photographing Aboriginals from Bendigo to Swan Hill. Parting ways with Batchelder, Creelman was left with the camera and the photographs were lost. Commissioned by the Americans Alexander Murray and Peleg Jackson to survey the Murray River from Albury to Goolwa, a 1750 miles journey, he achieved this in a canoe with an Aboriginal tracker and a dancing master named Everest; resulting in a 200 metres long chart on rollers, used by him as pilot of the *Lady Daly*. Pierce paints the Niagara Falls for the Niagara Hotel, Melbourne.

1864

In Adelaide he teaches Townsend Duryea the art of ambrotype.

1866

In May, he leaves Adelaide for Wentworth and becomes captain of the steamship *Lady Daly*.

1868

Augustus Baker Pierce (Jnr) born Balmain, NSW. Captains the steamer *Corowa* on the Murray and Darling Rivers.

1869

Captains the steamer *Jane Eliza*. In Echuca, Pierce paints 24 panoramas each canvas 6 foot by 9 foot, stitched together to make 212 foot panorama features American war scenes, and features of the Lower Murray River. These were presented by Pierce and his partner

Prince of Wales Theatre in Bathurst, with some of Gus Pierce's troupe.

Dodd's Hotel, Hill End 1872, with artist Gus Pierce, (third right).

George Kendall, with songs and comic banter. On November 19, Pierce married Agnes Carney at Moama, NSW.

1870

Herbert Edward Pierce born in Echuca. Pierce declared insolvent. Painted the Echuca Flood and Pierce then toured the panorama in a travelling showcase in NSW and Victoria over two years, painting murals for a hotel at Tibooburra. Also set up a bakery at Jawbone, near Dubbo.

1871

Captain of the Murray steamer *Jane Eliza*. Exhibited his panorama with music at Wagga Wagga. In June, exhibited the panorama at the Royal Assembly Rooms, and the Prince of Wales Theatre in Bathurst. Pierce's wife Agnes, and their two children Augustus and Herbert, join him in Bathurst. Exhibited the panorama at Cogden's Assembly Rooms in Gulgong in July and August, painted murals for the Bridge View Inn at Rylestone. New panorama of the Franco-Prussian War exhibited at the Prince of Wales Theatre, Bathurst in September and October, followed by two new scenes at the Royal Assembly Rooms, Bathurst on November 17. *A Voyage Around the World* plus new scenes based on the writings of Artemus Ward were shown at the Prince of Wales theatre on December 16

1872

Exhibited in Orange, but his paintings were ruined in transit. Created a huge tent theatre in Clarke Street, Hill End – 80 feet by 40 feet with 9 foot high corrugated-iron sides, performing with William B. Gill in a variety show, *Jumpers of Hill End*. Painted a life-size portrait of Bernhardt Holtermann with his famous nugget, and Holtermann provided Pierce with a studio at his Star of Hope mine. He painted murals for the Dodd's Hotel, Hill End.

1873

Holtermann encouraged Pierce to paint a new 200 foot panorama, *The Mirror of Life*. Equipped with a coach and horse Pierce and his

Gus Pierce, in doorway, his son Augustus at his feet, William B. Gill
(second right), Theatre Royal, Hill End 1872.

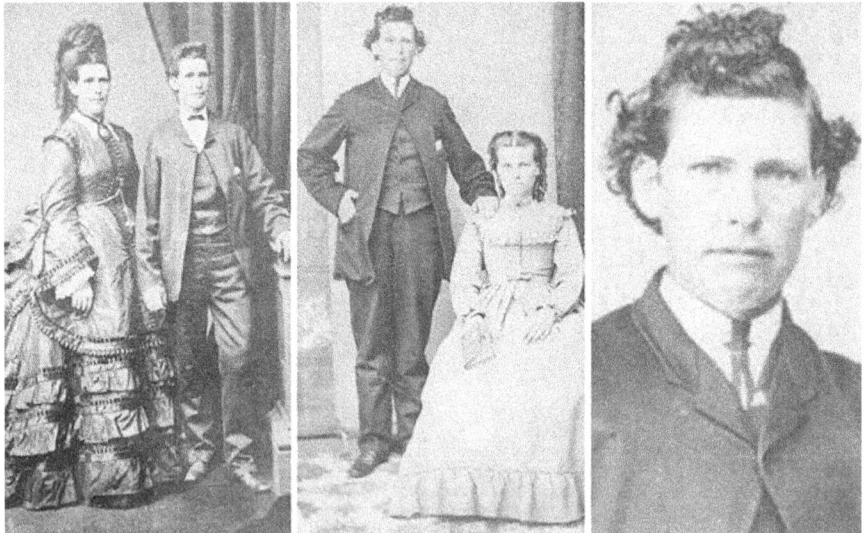

Ellen Tremayne, as De Lacy Evans, as she appeared in the 1880s.

family toured the panorama around NSW over the next two years. While Gill edited the *Hill End Observer*, Pierce had regular survey work during the mining boom

1874

Following the mining bust at Hill End, Pierce returned to the Murray, travelling the panoramas through difficult terrain, where much was destroyed. Captained the steamboat *Victoria*.

1875

Pierce decorated the Steampacket Hotel at Echuca and exhibits in Wagga Wagga, in the off-season, returning to the steamboat *Victoria*. He is also in charge of the *Lady Daly*.

1876

Pierce is Captain of the steamship *Riverina*.

1877

Family moved to Geelong.

1878

Completed a new *Mirror of Life* panorama, and painted horses and local sportsmen.

1879

Pierce painted a new Victorian panorama, drew cartoons for The Lantern, and was co-owner of *Le Figaro* in Adelaide. *The Mirror of Australia* panorama on display in Echuca.

1880

Exhibited the Victorian panorama while having a successful role in selling advertising at railway stations in the main cities, then toured the *Mirror of Life* to Geelong and Castlemaine, while operating a 'cigar divan' in Geelong.

1881

Pierce added the male impersonator, Ellen Tremayne (De Lacy Evans) to his touring troupe. The panorama left Australia and was shown in England.

The Metropolitan Meat Market (top) and a Meat Market personality (lower left) both painted by Gus Pierce. The Rose of Australia hotel, Melbourne.

1883

Pierce owned the Black Bull Hotel at Geelong, while living as an "animal artist" in Malop Street, Geelong with his family. At the Inn he painted 4 canvases 6 feet by five feet with Swiss and local scenes, while a painting 16 feet by 5 feet showed a football match on the Corio cricket ground.

1888

Painted on the Surf Coast Shire, showing Airey's Inlet lighthouse before it was completed. Painted banners for the Wharf Labourer's Union and Port Phillip Stevedore Labourer's Eight-hour Day Association.

1891

Purchased the Rose of Australia hotel in Melbourne, and his caricatures of Melbourne Meat Market personalities are in the State Library of Victoria as "Gus B. Pierce".

1892

Leaves Geelong in July and moved to Melbourne.

1893

Lived as an artist in Peel Street, Melbourne. His watercolour of the commercial meat market in North Melbourne is in the State Library of Victoria by "Augustus Baker Pierce". Agnes Pierce granted New Colonial Wine Licence.

1894

Agnes Pierce nee` Carney dies on 6 January 1894. Pierce was present on July 10 at the exhumation of Henry Needle and his two children, Elsie and May at Boorundara Cemetery, Richmond. This followed the poisoning case of Louis Juncken at the hands of Martha Needle. It was found that her husband and her deceased children had all presented the same symptoms, and in all cases—arsenic was found in sufficient quantities to cause death; and when the bodies were exhumed the Police had Pierce there as a photographer. Pierce tried his luck in the Western Australian gold fields before returning to USA.

Two of Pierce's drawings from the original edition of *Knocking About*.

1895

Departs Sydney on 20 August 1895, arriving in Vancouver, Canada on 14 September.

1921

Pierce's son Augustus Baker Pierce, died in Melbourne on May 1.

1924

Yale University Press published *Knocking About*, by Augustus Baker Peirce, edited by Mrs Albert Leadbeater, was funded by a foundation in memory of Curtis Seaman Read.

1935

Herbert Edward Pierce dies 14th June 1935. Neither of Gus Pierce's sons married or had any recorded children.

... upon returning from one of my trips I was obliged to take one of my boats and rescue my wife and small son from the second story of our house and remove them to the Town Hall ...

INDEX

Gus Pierce, with his son Augustus, outside the Tattersall's Hotel, Hill End.